Employee Stock Options – Executive Tax Planning

2026 Edition

Michael Gray, CPA with Thi T. Nguyen, CPA

Published by:
Silicon Valley Publishing Co.
2482 Wooding Ct.
San Jose, CA 95128-4271
United States of America
ISBN 978-1-7324865-9-1

For more information

Would your company like to educate its employees about tax rules for employee stock options?

Thi T. Nguyen, CPA is available for a limited number of presentations to employee groups about the tax rules for employee stock options and employee stock purchase plans. For more information, call write Thi T. Nguyen, CPA at ATL CPAs & Advisors, Inc. at thi@atlcpa.com, or 333 W. Santa Clara St., Ste. 620, San Jose, CA 95113

Want more detailed information?

This book is an introduction to issues for planning for employee stock options. Michael Gray has written a more detailed explanation of these rules in another book, *Secrets of Tax Planning For Employee Stock Options, Stock Grants and ESOPs.* You can get a copy at Amazon.com or www.employeestockoptionsecrets.com.

Table of Contents

Here's what Michael Gray's clients said

"Approximately 10 years ago, my company went through a round of investment causing a large portion of my stock options to be exercised. This caused an issue with tax treatments of the ISO stock and my local accountant informed me that I owed both AMT and regular income tax for a combined tax of over 60%. I was directed to my firm's large CPA firm who also said I owed a very large tax bill. I was desperate and Googled, finding Mike's credentials as an expert in these situations. That was on April 12th. On April 13th, Mike informed me that I did not owe such a large tax bill, and he saved me a large portion of my proceeds from the sale. I have trusted Mike ever since to have my taxes accurately prepared."

–Bob Kalish
Albertson, New York

"I exercised some incentive stock options during 2005 and had a substantial alternative minimum tax. Early in 2006, my employer was acquired, resulting in a disqualified disposition of my ISO stock.

"My local accountant wasn't familiar with handling something like ISO stock. A fellow employee at my company said you helped him with the same transaction, resulting in a big refund.

"Your firm prepared amended 2006 income tax returns, resulting in a recovery of most of the alternative minimum tax paid in 2005.

"The IRS selected the amended return for audit. I was impressed that the IRS agent said he researched the issue and found that Michael Gray, CPA was an expert on the subject of incentive stock options and alternative minimum tax, which the agent hadn't dealt with before!

"You explained what happened to the agent and provided requested documentation. With a minimum of hassles, our amended return was accepted as filed. The entire examination to report process took just slightly over two months.

"I would recommend your firm to anyone who has incentive stock options."

–Richard Gold
Carmel, New York

"To Whom It May Concern:

"I first met Mike Gray in 1999 to ask his assistance with stock option tax issues. Little did I know back then that over the next few years, Mike would help me with a hairy tax documentation problem, help my wife and me set up our will, provide me with advice on starting my new company, and become our company tax advisor. Along the way, Mike has provided me with excellent legal contacts and even sales reference materials.

"Adding it all up, you soon realize that Mike is much more than just a CPA – he is a very knowledgeable advisor and guide in all facets of our financial life. I'm very glad to count Mike Gray as one of my most trusted advisors."

Best Regards,
Dean

–Dean Haritos
Oakland, California

"Mike is a very astute tax professional. He has provided much guidance so that we can try and be as tax efficient as possible and keep as much of our hard earned dollars!"

–Suzanne and Scott Gardner

"There is something in Mike's DNA that makes him special at accounting. His ease with handling minutiae has enabled him to really save my butt!"

–John Mardinly

"Mr. Gray really knows his stock options and he is an expert with 'AMT' – Alternative Minimum Tax. Mr. Gray helped me receive a $94,988.00 credit towards my tax liability. The savings in penalty, interest and stress are worth much, much more. Thanks a $ million!"

–John Simon

And from the media …

"During the tech boom, Silicon Valley workers had surprisingly few places to turn for help with their stock options. Mike Gray was one of them, providing an authoritative voice of prudence in a time of irrational exuberance. Steeped in the complexities of tax laws and strategies, he was among the first to co-author a primer to help workers understand how options worked and how to take money off the table."

Mark Schwanhausser
Personal finance reporter
San Jose Mercury News
San Jose, California

Effective January 1, 2018, Ms. Thi T. Nguyen of ATL CPAs & Advisors, Inc. became the successor to Michael Gray, CPA's tax consulting and preparation firm. She is a partner at ATL CPAs & Advisors, Inc. and manages the tax services department for the firm. Thi worked with Michael Gray, CPA for ten years and has a masters in taxation degree. She has more than 24 years experience in public accounting. Michael Gray chose Thi as his successor because of his confidence in her ability to advise clients relating to employee stock issues and her tax return preparation skills.

Special Offer
Gift Certificate

ATL CPAs & Advisors inc

Gift Certificate

ATL CPAs & Advisors, Inc.

AMOUNT : $275 VALID UNTIL : 6/30/2026

333 W. Santa Clara St., Ste. 620, San Jose, CA 95113
THI@ATL-CPA.COM

1

Why Michael Gray is an invaluable resource for employee stock options

As a Certified Public Accountant and tax consultant in Silicon Valley, "stock options central," I have been helping executives plan for employee stock options as a practice focus since 1985.

I was working as a tax manager at KMG Main Hurdman (later acquired by KPMG Peat Marwick) and one of our clients, Viking Freight Systems, had a public offering. In the process of going public, the company hired professional management employees, and included employee stock options as part of their compensation package.

Ron Pelzel, then new president of Viking Freight, asked me to make a comparison of the different stock options available and how they work. I spent an enormous amount of time making a comparative table. Then I sent it to Douglas Lundell, the compensation specialist for KMG Main Hurdman.

Doug said something like, "You were crazy to do the project this way. You should have just copied an article from a tax conference. But, since you went to all this trouble, would you make a presentation on this subject to the firm's tax partners and managers?" So I participated in a panel on Compensation and Employee Benefits at a firm Tax Conference during October 1985.

After the presentation, several partners and managers told me they had never seen much information about employee stock options and that clients outside the West Coast weren't using them very much.

Little did we know that we were just in front of an explosion in the use of stock options!

I started disseminating information about options to clients of the firm.

In June 1986, I left KMG Main Hurdman and formed Hubler, Gray and Associates with G. Rich Hubler. Many of our broker friends referred clients with employee stock options. My friend, Dick Blakely, who then worked at Smith Barney, arranged for me to give a presentation to his clients. Some of the companies whose employees we helped included Acuson, Cisco Systems and JDS Uniphase.

In 1996, Rich and I disbanded our partnership and I started my own CPA firm, Michael Gray, CPA. My wife, Janet, took a computer class at West Valley College, and her teacher told her to encourage me to set up a web page. My daughter, Dawn, loves working with computers, so she helped me set up the site, one of the earliest for CPA firms in the United States. We set up an email newsletter and posted past newsletters, articles and questions and answers on our web site, many about employee stock options.

The web site proved to be a natural way to attract high technology executives with employee stock options. It was featured in an article, *Being There*, in the October 1997 issue of the *Journal of Accountancy* and on KNTV (television) news.

We then got into the "Roaring 90's," including a booming stock market and a rash of public offerings for "Dot Com" companies. Options became a form of currency. Companies even paid for their rent using stock options. A flood of employees with options came to me for advice.

In 2000, Gabriel Fenton, a stock broker, asked me to join with him and Joseph Stern III, another stock broker, to write a book. *Employee Stock*

Options – A Strategic Planning Guide for the 21st Century Optionaire was published during 2000.

At the end of 2000 and early 2001, the stock market crashed. An overwhelming rush of employees with option stock called for help. This was a tax disaster. I made a lot of referrals to other accountants because I couldn't handle them all.

At the suggestion of marketing guru Dan Kennedy, Dawn and I formed the Employee Stock Option Advisors Association, LLC (ESOAA). The first edition of our newsletter devoted to option issues was issued during December 2000.

We published a comprehensive reference manual, *Secrets of Tax Planning For Employee Stock Options* during 2001.

The timing was wrong for the Employee Stock Option Advisors Association. We never got a critical mass of professionals to participate. We liquidated ESOAA at the end of 2003 and converted the newsletter to *Michael Gray, CPA's Option Alert.* We continued publishing that newsletter until we discontinued it in 2018, when I sold my tax consulting and tax return preparation practice to Thi Nguyen. I continue explaining tax developments in my newsletter, *Michael Gray, CPA's Tax and Business Insight.* (You can subscribe by filling out the form at www.taxtrimmers.com.)

I have given many live seminars and telephone seminars to groups of employees and advisors. Just before Google went public, I was invited to speak and advise small groups of their employees.

I am in the process of issuing an updated edition of *Secrets of Tax Planning For Employee Stock Options,* which will be available to purchase at Amazon.com or www.employeestockoptionsecrets.com.

Since getting that book requires a significant investment and the information may be overwhelming for people who aren't tax or investment advisors, I decided to make a more basic book – this book.

Thanks to reporter Mark Schwanhausser, who has since left the *San Jose Mercury News*, we have been quoted in many local news articles over the years, including a beautiful interview, *CPA Helps Valley Workers Navigate Their Stock Options*, in the August 5, 2007 edition. I have also been quoted in many other publications, including *The Wall Street Journal*, *The New York Times*, and *The San Francisco Chronicle.*

In 2009, I started hosting a public access television show, *Financial Insider Weekly.* Among the episodes were interviews on employee stock options with options trader John Olagues and attorney Mary Russell. You can find the interviews on YouTube under "financialinsiderweek" or "@financialinsiderweekly". (I discontinued the show in September 2017.)

Despite changes in the tax laws and accounting disclosure laws that have made stock options much more expensive to offer to employees and option-related scandals at Enron and WorldCom, they continue to be a popular employee benefit.

Effective January 1, 2018, Ms. Thi T. Nguyen, CPA became the successor for my tax consulting and tax return preparation practice. Thi worked with me for ten years and has more than 24 years of public accounting experience. For an appointment, contact Thi at thi@atl-cpa.com. Be sure to tell her you read this book.

This book has been updated for changes adopted in the One Big Beautiful Bill Act of 2025.

Michael Gray, CPA
August 21, 2025

2

The Problem – The Busy Employee

With the demands of their work and family lives, many employees neglect giving attention to their finances. They expect that, if they work hard, their finances will automatically be handled.

Consequently, employees often just keep their heads down, taking care of daily "fire fighting," only to discover one day they face huge tax problems.

As many people experienced during the boom of the late 1990's and the busts of 2000, 2008, and 2020, there can be enormous swings of value in corporate stock in a relatively short time frame. An employee may be a paper millionaire one day and only have wallpaper the next.

The employee must set aside time to deal with these critical issues. His or her financial survival may be at stake.

After the 2000 technology market crash, I attended a "Town Hall" meeting where employees shared their tales of disaster from improperly handling stock options. Some had their entire net worth wiped out, and then some. People's health was ruined, including losing their hair from stress and worry. Funding for the education of their children was in doubt. Families were in danger of losing their homes.

This is serious stuff.

My guiding principle is, employee stock options and the related stock are investments. Once you have accumulated a significant value, sell the stock and get it diversified as soon as possible to preserve the value.

(Options trader John Olagues and John Summa offer alternative hedging strategies in their book, *Getting Started In Employee Stock Options*, published by John Wiley & Sons, Inc. I recommend that you also study that book.)

Don't take unnecessary risks regarding providing for the cash to pay taxes. If you don't otherwise have the cash to pay the taxes, sell stock sooner. You'll pay more tax, but be sure you have the funds to pay your tax bill.

If exercising an option is going to put you in a financial bind, such as during a lock out period or for non-traded stock of a private company, maybe it would be wiser to wait until the stock is liquid before exercising.

The stock market is a barometer of the emotional state of the economy. In the short term, you can't rely on the stock market behaving rationally.

There are two emotions that drive investment behavior – greed and fear. Greed can prevent people from taking their gains. They can ride a stock all the way up and all the way down. Fear can also result in making poor decisions. An executive may be afraid of what his or her peers may think if he or she sells his or her stock. Will they think I'm disloyal? Will they think I'm chicken? An employee may be afraid to sell a stock that has declined in value because it may recover.

During the market downturn of late 2000, I saw many people sell their ISO stock and repurchase it, trying to use the "escape hatch" and getting caught in the "wash sale" trap (see the chapter on incentive stock options), only to see the value of the repurchased shares go down and out.

The question is, from an investment point of view, "If this wasn't my employer's stock and if there were no tax considerations, would I buy and hold this stock right now anyway?" If the answer is "No," you are probably better off not buying and holding the stock. Don't let the tax tail wag the dog!

3

Diversification

Almost all of the employees with stock options or option stock that I do planning for initially have a heavy investment concentration in employer stock. Their employer stock and options usually represent their single major investment, sometimes second only to their residence.

This position defies common sense.

Many employees have an emotional investment in their employer's stock. Because of their emotional investment, their judgment is clouded and they make irrational decisions in managing the stock as an investment. The consequences can be disastrous.

Investment concentration can make sense as a strategy to build wealth. (See Robert Kiyosaki's book, *Rich Dad, Poor Dad.*) In this situation, you are taking a risk with the hope of achieving a big return. You can reduce your cash exposure during this period by not exercising your options, but there is a tax cost for doing this, explained in the various chapters on the specific types of options. Eventually you may be forced to exercise "in the money" options that are going to expire.

Once you have achieved some measure of value, it makes sense to protect it. The way I explain this to clients is, "Congratulations! You've won the lottery! You have read the stories of people who have won the lottery before, haven't you? What do they end up with in a few years?

Nothing! You need to take steps to assure that, at the end of the road, you still have something."

I believe that people with a large value of employer stock and stock options need to adopt a program of orderly liquidation and diversification. When clients are reticent to part with their employer stock, I encourage them to sell at least half as soon as possible. (By the way, large corporate owners like Bill Gates and Larry Ellison regularly sell blocks of their stock under the direction of their investment managers.)

(Options trader John Olagues and John Summa offer alternative hedging strategies in their book, *Getting Started In Employee Stock Options*, published by John Wiley & Sons, Inc. I recommend that you also study that book. Be aware the hedging strategies, such as buying an offsetting put for the company shares, could "spoil" the holding period for an ISO or ESPP. Consult with a tax advisor who is familiar with those rules.)

Some of my clients or prospective clients tell me that they have diversified investments. Then I learn their entire portfolios consist of stocks of high technology companies. This means that all of their portfolio is in one *asset class*. An asset class tends to have the same market movements up and down, so they are not getting much protection from this strategy.

Instead, the investor should be dividing the portfolio among various asset classes. Some asset classes include short-term bonds, domestic large capitalization industrial companies, offshore middle capitalization companies, and others. This approach to investing, called *modern portfolio theory*, is used by large retirement trusts that need to have a defined investment policy. Modern portfolio theory was developed by two economists, Harry Markowitz and William Sharpe. To learn more about it, read *Craig Martin on Asset Class Investing* by Craig Martin (www.fwcg.net or info@fwcg.net) or *Risk-Return Analysis* by Harry M. Markowitz.

Some stockbrokers don't really know how risk-managed investing works. They are just pushing the latest "hot stocks," including initial public offerings underwritten by their brokerage firms. If you enjoy Las Vegas style gambling, it's OK to budget some "play money" for this type of activity. But this is not the way your "nest egg" should be managed.

Learn about modern portfolio theory and find an investment manager to help you implement it for your own investment portfolio.

4

Incentive Stock Options

Incentive Stock Options (ISOs) are a form of compensation that have been particularly popular in Silicon Valley. This reflects the dynamic nature of our local economy, which emphasizes growing new businesses. During the 2000's, the IRS issued guidelines for pricing options, the accounting authorities changed stock option disclosure rules and the federal government enacted Sarbannes Oxley, increasing burdens on new businesses from Sarbannes-Oxley. These developments may create barriers for issuing new ISOs.

The Tax Cuts and Jobs Act of 2017 (TCJA) increased the exemptions for the alternative minimum tax, eliminated many deductions that were alternative minimum tax preferences and created an election to defer tax when exercising employee stock options of certain companies whose stock isn't publicly traded.

The One Big Beautiful Bill Act of 2025 (OBBBA) generally made the TCJA changes for tax rates and the alternative minimum tax, which were scheduled to expire after 2025, permanent, creating more certainty for long-term planning. OBBBA includes many phaseouts for various tax benefits, such as the deduction for state income taxes and real estate taxes, making tax planning more complex. "Permanent" means the OBBBA provisions will remain effective until Congress changes them in the future.

What are the tax and economic benefits of incentive stock options?

An employee may control shares of corporate stock for a limited time for no investment. Therefore, the employee may enjoy potential capital appreciation with no out-of-pocket cash risk.

When the stock has appreciated and the employee exercises an incentive stock option to purchase the stock, no taxable income is currently recognized for the excess of the fair market value of the stock over the purchase price (or "spread"). The "spread" is considered a tax preference in computing the alternative minimum tax, discussed later.

The "spread" at exercise may be taxed when the stock is sold as a long-term capital gain, provided the holding period rules are met. In order to qualify for long-term capital gain treatment, the stock must be held more than two years after the date of grant and more than one year after the date of exercise. The tax rates that apply to the gain are discussed below. The date of grant is the date on which the board of directors or the stock option committee completes the corporate action constituting an offer of stock pursuant to the terms of the option, rather than the date on which the option agreement is prepared. The date of exercise is the date on which the grantor corporation receives notice of exercise of the option and payment for the stock, rather than the date the shares of stock are actually transferred.

If the holding period requirement is not met, the lesser of the "spread" at exercise or the gain from the sale of the stock is taxable as ordinary compensation income. (See also the discussion below "about early exercise provisions" for a different rule.) The gain on sale limitation is not available for a transaction where a loss would not be recognized, such as a wash sale, a transfer to a charitable remainder trust, or a sale to a related party.

Since the maximum federal income tax rate that applies to long-term capital gains may be 15%, 20% or 23.8%, meeting the holding period requirements may be important for employees who are planning with respect to incentive stock options.

If ordinary income results from not meeting the holding period requirements, the employer will receive a tax deduction for the "compensation" element with no cash outlay required.

A tax law has been passed that makes it clear that the exercise of an ISO is not subject to withholding of Social Security or Medicare employment taxes and also not subject to withholding of federal income taxes.

What rates of tax apply for long-term capital gains?

Long-term capital gains rates generally apply to sales of securities held more than one year.

The tax brackets for ordinary taxable income are indexed for inflation. For 2025, maximum federal tax rates apply to married persons filing joint returns with taxable income exceeding $751,600; $375,800 for married, filing separate returns; and $626,350 for heads of households and single persons. The maximum federal tax rate for ordinary income is 37%.

The 2025 maximum federal tax rate is 20% for qualifying long-term capital gains and qualified dividends when taxable income exceeds $600,050 for married persons filling joint returns, $300,000 for married, filing separate returns, $566,700 for heads of households, and $533,400 for single persons.

See the discussion about the net investment income tax below. This additional tax can increase the maximum federal income tax rate for long-term capital gains to 23.8%. Phase outs for other tax benefits can raise the effective rate even higher.

The federal tax rate for long-term capital gains when taxable income is below the maximum rate thresholds listed above is generally 15%.

Individuals in the 10% and 15% tax brackets may qualify for a 0% tax rate for long-term capital gains.

With a variety of income thresholds having different tax effects, including phase outs of tax benefits, it will be important to make tax projections when planning for exercising incentive stock options. Taxpayers might have other decisions to make, such as whether to sell other stock, whether to defer compensation, or whether to make a Roth conversion. Working with a tax advisor who uses tax projection software that has been updated for the latest tax law changes makes sense to discuss the interplay of these matters in tax planning.

Alternative minimum tax. The same maximum rates for long-term capital gains apply for computing the alternative minimum tax. (See below.)

What is the net investment income tax?

The net investment income tax (NII tax) is a separate 3.8% surtax on the lesser of "net investment income" or the excess of "modified" adjusted gross income over $250,000 ($125,000 for married taxpayers filing separate income tax returns). Since the NII tax is a separate surtax, it isn't included in the "regular tax" amount when computing the minimum tax credit. (See below for an explanation of the alternative minimum tax.)

The ordinary income from the disqualified disposition of stock acquired by exercising an incentive stock option is considered to be "wages" and is not included in net investment income. These "wages" are also statutorily excluded from income subject to employment taxes like Social Security and Medicare taxes. This is an advantage of ordinary income from a disqualified disposition of an incentive stock option compared to an exercise of a nonqualified stock option.

Most long-term capital gains from securities sales, including long-term capital gains from a qualified sale of stock acquired from exercising an incentive stock option, are considered investment income for computing the NII tax.

What is the alternative minimum tax and how does it relate to planning for exercising incentive stock options?

The Federal income tax incorporates two ways of computing tax. There is a "regular" tax that most of us are fairly familiar with. There is also an "alternative minimum tax" (AMT). Tax is computed using both methods, and you generally pay the higher tax. If the alternative minimum tax does apply, a portion of the excess over the regular tax may be available as a tax credit in a later year, treated somewhat like a prepayment of the later year's tax.

For 2025, the alternative minimum tax rates for single persons and married persons filing joint income tax returns are 26% for the first $239,100 of alternative minimum taxable income (AMTI) and 28% for AMT income over $239,100. The threshold for married persons filing separate returns is $119,500. The maximum rates as described above for the regular tax for sales of capital assets also apply for the alternative minimum tax.

The AMT exemption and phaseouts are adjusted annually for inflation. For 2025, single persons and heads of households have an AMT exemption of $88,100 phased out by 25% of the excess of AMTI over $626,350, and eliminated for AMTI of $978,750 or more. The AMT exemption on a joint return for married persons for 2025 is $137,000, phased out by 25% of the excess of AMTI over $1,252,700, and eliminated for AMTI of $1,800,700 or more.

Effective for tax years beginning after 2025, OBBBA will slightly modify the back year annual inflation adjustments for the exemption amounts. The thresholds for phasing out the exemptions will be reset to $1 million for 2026 for married persons, filing joint returns and $500,000 for 2026 for single persons and heads of households, indexed for inflation for future years. The exemption phaseout rate will be increased from 25% to 50%, so the exemption is phased out twice as fast under the new law.

The alternative minimum tax is a critical concern relating to ISOs. The excess of the fair market value on the date of exercise over the option price is considered a "tax preference" that is added to regular taxable income in computing the alternative minimum taxable income (AMTI) for the year of exercise. Note the reduced tax rates for long-term capital gains do not apply to this "spread" amount for the year of exercise, because they are taxed as ordinary income. In the past, major deductions were disallowed for AMT, including state income taxes, property taxes, most miscellaneous itemized deductions and personal exemption deductions. With the TCJA limitation for regular tax reduced to $10,000 ($5,000 for married, filing separate returns) for state income taxes and property taxes, the repeal of 2% miscellaneous itemized deductions and the repeal of personal exemptions, more taxpayers will be able to avoid the alternative minimum tax for modest ISO exercises. It's even more important that tax planning computations be made when exercising an ISO.

OBBBA has made the tax deduction changes of the TCJA permanent, with some changes. Effective for 2025, the deduction for state income taxes and property taxes (SALT) is increased to $40,000 ($20,000 for married, filing a separate return). For 2026, the deduction will be $40,400 ($20,200 for married, filing a separate return). The ceiling will be increased to 101% of the previous year amount for 2027 through 2029, and revert to $10,000 ($5,000 for married filing a separate return) after 2029.

The SALT cap is reduced to no less than the $10,000 ($5,000 for married, filing a separate return) or the actual amount, if less, by 30% of the excess of the taxpayer's modified gross income over $500,000 ($250,000 for married, filing separately) for 2025, and $505,000 ($252,500 for married filing separately) for 2026. The SALT cap phaseout threshold will be increased to 101% of the dollar amount in effect for the previous year for 2027 to 2029.

In addition, since the tax rate that applies in computing the AMT (26-28%) may exceed the tax rate that applies to certain long-term capital gains (20% or 15%), the application of the AMT credit might not be "matched" with the tax applying at the sale of the stock. Also recall from the discussion above that the minimum tax credit can't be applied to reduce the 3.8% net investment income tax (NII tax) on long-term capital gains from a qualified disposition of ISO shares. The alternative minimum tax credit could represent a prepayment of tax for several years and might not be recovered at all.

The difference between the maximum regular federal income tax rate, 37%, and the maximum AMT rate, 28% is now 9%. The TCJA and OBBBA increase in the maximum rate for long-term capital gains, including the net investment income tax, to 23.8% has reduced the tax benefits of incentive stock options.

Congress enacted relief in the form of refundable minimum tax credits for taxpayers who were unable to recoup their alternative minimum tax credits due to the market crash in 2000. That relief expired after 2012.

THE TAX BENEFIT OF HOLDING THE STOCK FOR A CURRENT EXERCISE WITH A LARGE AMT GAIN USUALLY DOESN'T ADEQUATELY COMPENSATE FOR THE RISK. IN OUR CURRENT TAX ENVIRONMENT, MANY EMPLOYEES SHOULD SELL THE STOCK WHEN THEY EXERCISE ISOS WHEN THE STOCK IS PUBLICLY TRADED.

As an example of how the AMT is computed, John Smith, a single person, exercised an ISO in 2025, resulting in a tax preference of $300,000 for the "spread" at exercise. John did not sell the stock before the end of 2025. Here are his regular tax and AMT computations:

Regular tax:

Salary	$200,000
Interest income	2,000
Adjusted Gross Income	$202,000
Home mortgage interest	(25,000)
California income tax and real estate tax	(25,000)
Itemized deductions	(50,000)
Taxable income	$152,000
Regular tax	$ 29,324

Alternative minimum tax:

"Regular" AGI	$202,000
ISO adjustment	300,000
AMT AGI	$502,000
Home mortgage interest	(25,000)
AMT exemption	(88,100)
Taxable income for AMT	$388,900
Tentative AMT	$104,110
Regular tax	(29,324)
Alternative minimum tax	$ 74,786

The tax preference amount added to AMTI in the year of exercise is subtracted from AMTI in the year of sale as a basis adjustment. (It's added to the cost of the stock on AMT Schedule D.)

For example, Jane Employee exercises an ISO for Supergrow Corp stock on January 1, 20X1 (more than one year after the grant date). The option price is $100, and the fair market value of the stock on the date of exercise is $100,100. Therefore, Jane adds $100,000 to AMTI for the ISO tax preference. (This item is entered on the "incentive stock options" line of Form 6251.)

On January 15, 20X2, Jane sells the Supergrow stock she acquired with the ISO in 20X1 for $150,000. Jane subtracts $100,000 from AMTI as a basis adjustment. (This item is entered on the "adjusted gain or loss" line of Form 6251.) She might also be able to reduce her 20X2 tax using a minimum tax credit carryover from 20X1. Since the basis adjustment is reflected on an alternative minimum tax Schedule D, the adjustment could be subject to another limitation for a capital loss, so the basis adjustment for the year of sale could be less than $100,000 if the stock price drops.

If the employee sells the shares acquired using an ISO on the date the option is exercised, there is no AMTI adjustment because the spread between the fair market value on the date of exercise and the option price is reported as compensation income for regular tax reporting purposes.

The "wash sale" rules may impact an early disposition of shares acquired from exercising an ISO. If the employee acquires company stock or an option to purchase the stock within 30 days before or 30 days after selling company stock in an early disposition, the transaction may not qualify for the special treatment for dispositions in the year of exercise. The wash sale rule could apply for stock purchased on the open market, acquired by exercising an employee stock option, or acquired through an employee stock purchase plan or the purchase or grant of another stock option. Consider consulting with a tax advisor to get more details about how this may affect your tax planning.

As I suggested above, the alternative minimum tax that results from timing differences, such as the ISO adjustment, is carried over and may be used as a tax credit in a later year when the regular tax exceeds the AMT. No tax credit is allowed for the AMT that results from disallowed deductions, such as property taxes and state income taxes.

Adjustments relating to the disallowed deductions just mentioned could actually result in the AMT credit for timing differences "disappearing." (Note at line 18 on Form 8801 (AMT credit form) for 2025 that if the minimum tax on exclusion items exceeds the alternative minimum tax from the previous year's tax return, *the adjustment is entered as a negative amount.*) This will typically happen when there is a negative adjustment on the previous year's tax return for an ISO disposition, resulting in zero AMT. For more details on how your AMT credit can disappear, see our article, "The Amazing Disappearing AMT Credit" at http://www.stockoptionadvisors.com/stock/articles/disappearing-amt-credit/

Since many of these items have been repealed or severely limited under the TCJA and OBBBA, this will not be as big of a problem unless Congress restores the deductions in the future.

One of the services CPAs can provide is to estimate how many shares can be exercised by an employee without incurring an alternative minimum tax. The approach is to compute the point where the AMT equals the regular tax. In those cases where the spread for the options is a large value, this strategy isn't much help. Also, some high-income taxpayers could already be subject to the AMT even if they don't exercise ISOs.

Don't let the "tax tail wag the dog" when planning these transactions. The objective is to maximize what you keep. Don't walk away from a substantial gain just because it results in a tax.

AMT considerations can force an employee to sell shares of stock to generate the cash needed to pay income taxes. Alternatively, the employee could borrow the amount needed to pay the tax using a margin loan secured by the stock. (The interest is not deductible for a loan when the proceeds are used to pay personal income taxes.)

Planning to exercise ISOs.

There are a number of considerations in planning to exercise ISOs.

If the employee has some latitude in timing when the ISOs may be exercised, then a computation may be made to compare the AMT with the regular tax to minimize the AMT liability.

Stock that is identical to the stock to be received may be exchanged at face value to pay the exercise price when exercising ISOs as a tax-free exchange. The old shares are surrendered in payment for the new shares, and no taxable gain or loss is reported for the transaction. This is called "pyramiding" or a "swap." However, stock acquired by exercising an ISO that hasn't yet been held for the required period will not qualify for this type of exchange. According to IRS regulations, when an employee makes a swap to exercise an ISO and shares are sold before the holding period requirements are met, shares for which ordinary income would be recognized are considered sold first. (Treasury Regulations Section 1.422-5(b)(2).)

For example, Jane employee has 100 shares of Supergrow stock with a total fair market value of $5,000 ($50 per share), for which she paid $50, or $.50 per share. She has an incentive stock option to purchase 5,000 shares of Supergrow stock for $1 per share. If Supergrow permits it, Jane may surrender her 100 shares and receive 5,000 shares in return. Her tax basis in the shares received will be $.50 per share, the basis of the shares surrendered, for 100 of the shares and zero for 4,900 shares. She will have no taxable gain or loss for the exchange. She will still report a tax preference of $250,000 (value of shares received) - $5,000 (option price) = $245,000 in computing the alternative minimum tax for the year of exercise and her AMT tax basis for the 4,900 additional shares will be $245,000 / 4,900 = $50 per share.

Ultimately, economics must rule. When options are going to lapse that represent significant assets, you should exercise them despite the tax results. (If the stock is of a privately-held company that can't be sold, the cash requirement to pay the option price plus alternative minimum taxes could make exercising an ISO prohibitive when it has a high value. In some cases, employees have had to "walk away" from exercising most of their options because they couldn't afford to pay the option price plus the tax. See below about the new election to defer gain for the exercise of an employee stock option of privately-held companies.)

Limited tax relief for some private company stock options and stock grants.

Employees with stock-based compensation with employer companies that aren't publicly traded have always had a problem with having taxable compensation without receiving or having access to cash to pay the related income taxes.

The Tax Cuts and Jobs Act includes some tax relief for this situation, effective for options exercised and RSUs settled after December 31, 2017.

Certain employees can make an election under amended Internal Revenue Code Section 83(i) to defer recognition of the amount of income for qualified stock transferred to the employee by the employer. The election is effective for income tax purposes, not for computing FICA (Social Security and Medicare) or FUTA taxes.

The election must be made no later than 30 days after the first time the employee's right to the stock is substantially vested or is transferable, whichever occurs earlier.

When the election is made, the income is taxable for the earliest tax year that includes:

1. The first date the qualified stock becomes transferable, including, for this purpose, to the employer.
2. The date the employee first becomes an "excluded employee". An excluded employee is an individual (i) who is a one-percent owner of the corporation at any time during the 10 preceding

calendar years; (ii) who is, or has been at any prior time, the chief executive officer or chief financial officer of the corporation or an individual acting in either capacity; (iii) who is a family member of an individual described in (i) or (ii), or (iv) who has been one of the four highest-compensated officers of the corporation for any of the 10 preceding tax years.

3. The first date on which any stock of the employer becomes readily tradable on an established securities market.
4. The date five years after the first date the employee's right to the stock becomes substantially vested; or
5. The date on which the employee revokes his or her election.

If the election is made relating to a "statutory option" (ISO or ESPP), the option will no longer be treated as a statutory option but treated as a nonqualified stock option.

The employer's deduction for the related compensation is also deferred until the employee is taxable for the income.

The election applies for qualified stock of an eligible corporation. A corporation is eligible for a tax year if: (1) no stock of the employer corporation or any predecessor is readily tradable on an established securities market during any preceding calendar year; and (2) the corporation has a written plan under which, in the calendar year, *not less than 80% of all employees who provide services to the corporation in the US or any US possession* are granted stock options or restricted stock units (RSUs) with the same rights and privileges to receive qualified stock.

Employers are subject to notice, withholding and reporting requirements for the election. The IRS is given discretion to provide transitional relief for these requirements and will issue guidelines for them.

Note that key shareholders won't get any relief and the participation requirements are very broad, which means this election may not really have a wide application. New stock compensation plans will have to be created to meet the requirements.

Planning to sell the stock.

The tax considerations are only a factor in making a decision to sell stock received by exercise of ISOs. Tax results of different scenarios should be estimated. What is the benefit from the maximum capital gains rate? What is the interrelation of gains to be reported, alternative minimum tax credits that are carried forward, tax preference adjustments from exercising ISOs and deductions that are disallowed for the AMT, such as state income taxes?

There are also tax accounting issues involved. Tracking multiple blocks of stock in a street (brokerage) account can be very complex. The general rule for tax reporting purposes is shares that can't be identified are accounted for on a first-in, first-out basis. A taxpayer can overcome this rule by giving the broker written instructions to sell specific blocks of stock, such as "sell the 500 shares of Supercorp Stock that I acquired on April 15, 20X1." Identifying shares sold as those with the highest tax basis can result in a substantial reduction of the current income tax. (See also above under "Planning to exercise ISOs" about the ordering rule for stock received in a tax-free exchange when exercising an ISO.)

Some employers provide their employees with reports with the information they need to report these transactions on their income tax returns.

Employers rely on their employees for notification about sales and transfers that result in compensation to be reported on the employee's W-2 and deducted on the employer's income tax return. The employer will need to know the date the option was exercised, the date of sale, the option price, the fair market value on the date of exercise, and if the value of the stock has declined after the date of exercise, the sale price of the stock. If the employee sells shares shortly after exercising an ISO, while holding shares previously acquired, the compensation amount could be reported in error. The employee must be careful or multiple tax adjustments could result (in short, a mess)!

For example, Jane Employee exercises an ISO for 100 shares of Supercorp on January 1, 20X2. She previously purchased 100 shares of Supercorp on the open market on June 30, 20X1. Jane sells 100 shares of Supercorp from her brokerage account on July 1, 20X2. Jane believes she sold the shares she acquired using her ISO, so she notifies her employer about the transaction, resulting in $10,000 being added to her compensation income for 20X2. However, since Jane did not give her broker any specific instructions as to which shares were sold, for income tax reporting she has actually sold the shares she acquired on June 30, 20X1, and should be reporting a long-term gain or loss with respect to those shares and no compensation income with respect to the ISO shares for 20X2.

The economic considerations are more important than the tax considerations when making decisions about selling stock. Having almost all of your investment portfolio in one stock exposes you to unnecessary and unwise market risk. Once you have built wealth, it's wise to protect it through diversification. As the old saying goes, "Pigs get fat, hogs get slaughtered!" The reduced rates applying to long-term capital gains for stock held more than 12 months may result in more reticence in adopting early diversification strategies. Since the alternative minimum tax will probably be controlling, this may be a mistake. The AMT is an additional investment that increases the risk of holding the stock.

Cash flow requirements may also dictate the sale of stock, including the requirement to pay taxes (including alternative minimum taxes). Timing the sale according to when the tax payments are required can result in deferring or postponing the tax, enabling the employee to squeeze out additional investment income.

Estimated tax considerations.

The employee should avoid potential penalties for underpayment of estimated tax or underwithholding by monitoring their estimated tax deposits and withholding.

Generally, for federal tax purposes, taxpayers must deposit at least their last year's tax in order to have "protected estimates." Individuals with adjusted gross income for the prior tax year of more than $150,000

($75,000 for married, filing separately) must deposit at least 110% of the prior year's tax to have "protected estimates."

The same estimated tax rules apply for California, provided the taxpayer's adjusted gross income doesn't exceed $1 million

Paying the tax through withholding instead of estimated tax payments has the advantage of being considered paid evenly throughout the year for making underpayment penalty computations, even if most of the withholding was actually done at the end of the year.

(Some states, including California, don't have "protected estimates" in some circumstances. For example, in California, taxpayers who have more than $1 million of adjusted gross income are required to pay estimated taxes based on the income for the current year. See your tax advisor for details.)

Disqualifying "early" transfers.

In some cases, transfers that are not actually sales of stock may result in a tax when the stock doesn't meet the holding period requirements. In these situations, the ordinary income for the "compensation" element will be reported by the employee for the year of transfer.

For example, gifts of the stock to a family member or a charity before meeting the holding period requirements will result in taxable income.

As previously mentioned, an exchange of the stock in a "swap" transaction will also result in taxable income.

Short sales of the stock or certain "collar" arrangements for the stock will also be treated as taxable transfers.

Holding period suspended.

Certain "hedging" transactions will suspend the holding period for the stock, extending the time required to meet the holding period requirements. Examples include buying an offsetting put, selling "deep in the money" calls "covered" by the stock, and "collar" arrangements that aren't considered to be sales.

Early exercise provisions.

Some employers permit employees to exercise their incentive stock options before they are vested. The stock received is subject to repurchase by the company at the option price if the employee leaves before the vesting requirements are met.

This can help employees to meet the holding period requirements sooner and reduce the tax preference from exercise.

The IRS has stated in final regulations that a Section 83(b) election can't be made for regular tax purposes when an ISO is exercised, because Section 83 isn't applicable at that time. The employee receives a tax benefit, because the holding period to qualify for long-term capital gain for regular tax reporting starts on the exercise date. The employee will avoid ordinary income reporting, despite the fact the stock is non-vested, provided the stock is held more than one year after the exercise date and more than two years after the grant date of the ISO. (Final Regulations Section 1.422-1(b)(2), Example 2.)

There is also a regular tax disadvantage of disallowing the Section 83(b) election for an early exercise of an ISO. If there is a disqualifying disposition of ISO stock, the ordinary income for unvested stock will be measured based on the excess of the fair market value over the option price *on the vesting date*, not the date of exercise. *If the employee is planning to make a disqualifying disposition of the stock, there is no advantage to making an early exercise of an ISO*. The employee might receive more tax benefits from an early exercise of an NQO with a Section 83(b) election than from an early exercise of an ISO with a disqualified disposition.

Since the tax benefits of ISOs don't apply for the alternative minimum tax, a Section 83(b) election can be made (and should be seriously considered) for alternative minimum tax purposes.

The general rule (under Section 83) when an employee receives restricted property (unvested stock) relating to his or her employment is the property received is valued when the restrictions lapse. When an employee makes a Section 83(b) election, he or she is electing to have the restrictions disregarded and the property valued on the date received.

The election must be made within 30 days of exercising the option (certified mail is recommended). It is sent to the Internal Revenue Service, and a copy is given to the employer. The IRS issued final regulations (T.D. 9779) eliminating the requirement that a copy of the Section 83(b) election be attached to the taxpayer's income tax return for the year of exercise.

The IRS has issued Form 15620 to be used to make the Section 83(b) election. Alternatively, the taxpayer may provide the same information to the IRS without the form.

For example, Peach Company permits employees to exercise their ISOs early. Peach is planning an initial public offering of its stock in six months, so the employees exercise their options early. The option price is $1. The estimated fair market value at exercise is $2. When the stock is vested after the IPO, the stock is trading at $100. If an employee makes a Section 83(b) election, his or her alternative minimum tax preference will be $1 per share. If an employee does not make the election, his or her alternative minimum tax preference will be $99 per share.

Note that if an employee forfeits stock after making a Section 83(b) election, such as for a termination, no loss will be allowed on the alternative minimum tax Schedule D with respect to the income reported on the exercise.

For example, John Employee is allowed to make an early exercise of ISOs for 100 shares of Peach Company stock, and does so on January 1, 20X1. The option price for the stock was $1 per share and the fair market value of the stock on the date of exercise was $10 per share. John makes a Section 83(b) election with respect to the exercise. John reports $900 for additional income on his AMT Form 6251 for 20X1. On January 1, 20X2, John is terminated and has to forfeit the shares, which are still unvested, to Peach Company. On his 20X2 AMT Schedule D, John is only allowed to report a loss of $100, and there is no gain or loss adjustment reported with respect to the forfeiture on John's 20X2 AMT Form 6251.

Disallowed compensation deductions for publicly-traded corporations

The tax deduction for compensation of certain key executives of public corporations is limited to $1 million per year. In the past, compensation relating to employee stock options was excluded from this limitation as "performance-based compensation."

Effective for tax years beginning after December 31, 2017, the exception for "performance-based compensation" has been repealed. There is a grandfather rule for written plans that were in effect on November 2, 2017, and that are not modified in any material respect on or after that date. The limit applies to any employee of a publicly held corporation who (1) is the principal executive officer (PEO) of the corporation, or acting in that capacity, at any time during the tax year; (2) is the principal financial officer (PFO) of the corporation, or acting in that capacity, at any time during the tax year; (3) is one of the three highest compensated officers for the tax year (other than the PEO or PFO); or was a covered employee of the corporation or any predecessor for any prior tax year beginning on or after January 1, 2017.

Effective for tax years beginning after December 31, 2025, OBBBA has extended the limitation to an allocated portion of $1,000,000 for a covered employee of a publicly-traded member of a controlled group. (An overall $1,000,000 deduction limit applies for the group.)

This limitation could result in the disallowance of significant deductions of compensation relating to the exercise of stock options.

What are the tax consequences for backdated options?

Here are four tax issues of concern for backdated options:

First, incentive stock options (ISOs) and employee stock purchase plans (ESPPs) may only be granted to employees. (IRC §§ 422(a)(2), 423(a)(2).) If the employer backdated the employee's start date, the individual may not have actually been an eligible employee. Therefore, the option will not qualify as an ISO or ESPP, and will be taxed as a non-qualified stock option.

Second, ISOs and ESPPs are required to be priced based on the fair market value on the grant date (or exercise date for ESPPs). (IRC §§ 422(b)(4), 423(b)(6).) If the option fails the pricing test on the actual grant date, it will be taxed according to the rules for non-qualified stock options.

Third, if a stock option has an option price less than the fair market value on the grant date, the option is probably subject to the rules for non-qualified stock options under § 409A. (Treasury regulations § 1.409A-1(b)(5)(i)(A).) This means the income from the option will be subject to a 20% penalty tax plus interest.

Fourth, a stock option with an option price less than the fair market value on the grant date won't qualify as "performance-based compensation" for the $1 million limitation of deduction of compensation paid to a covered employee of a publicly-held corporation. (Regs § 1.162-27(e)(2)(vi)(A).) Effective for tax years beginning before January 1, 2018, the limit applies to the CEO and the four highest-paid officers other than the CEO. Applying the limitation would result in the disallowance of significant deductions of compensation relating to exercising stock options. For tax years beginning after December 31, 2017, see the above discussion, "Disallowed compensation deductions expanded for publicly-traded corporations."

Insider issues.

Corporate insider issues are beyond the scope of this discussion.

Relatively recent changes in the securities laws have removed most of the restrictions on key executives for stock received by exercise of an incentive stock option.

The IRS has not updated an older ruling that indicates the restrictions under securities law Section 16(b) are a substantial risk of forfeiture. It may be an "insider" should file an election under Internal Revenue Code Section 83(b) (explained above) to fix the date to determine the "spread" adjustment for the exercise of the ISO. Otherwise, the date could be postponed by 6 months. Remember, the election should be made within **30 days** after exercising the option.

Conclusion.

An employee who tries to manage ISOs without professional assistance is taking a big, unnecessary risk. It is well worth the investment in professional fees to get professional guidance in navigating the treacherous labyrinth of the tax laws and help make sound investment decisions.

5

Non-Qualified Stock Options

Non-qualified stock options are a form of equity-based compensation that grew in popularity with the "go - go" economy of the 1990s. Although the benefits to employees are not as great as those for incentive stock options, employers have considerably more latitude in using non-qualified options. In addition, non-qualified stock options can be used to compensate people who aren't employees.

With the corporate governance rules under Sarbannes Oxley, financial reporting disclosure rules, bad publicity for back-dated stock options, and pricing guidelines as a result of legislation for non-qualified deferred compensation plans, the costs of granting employee stock options have dramatically increased. Despite the increased costs, companies continue to grant them – especially high technology start-up companies.

Since non-qualified stock options are a form of non-cash compensation, *exercising them can result in taxable income without having the cash to pay the tax.*

What are the economic advantages of using non-qualified options to an employer?

An employer is able to compensate employees and other service providers with no out-of-pocket costs (except employer taxes). The employer grants a right to acquire stock at a stated price. If the value of the stock exceeds the option price when exercised, the employer receives a tax deduction for the "spread." Under Internal Revenue Code Section 163(m), the deduction for compensation from employee stock options for certain key employees may be limited. See the discussion under " Disallowed compensation deductions expanded for publicly-traded corporations", below.

What are the economic advantages of using non-qualified options to an employee or service provider?

The recipient of a non-qualified option is able to enjoy the "upside" benefit of stock appreciation without the "downside" risk of stock value declines, because the recipient has the ability to exercise the option at a fixed price, but doesn't have to make a cash investment until the option is exercised.

For example, Sandra receives a non-qualified option to purchase 100 shares of Apple stock at $10 per share. Six months later, Apple stock has declined to $5 per share. Sandra has no out of pocket cost, so she has lost no cash.

One year later, Apple stock increases to $20 per share. Sandra exercises her option. She receives $2,000 of stock for a $1,000 cash investment, realizing an economic gain of $1,000.

What are the tax results of receiving a non-qualified stock option?

No taxable income usually results when an employee or service provider receives a non-qualified stock option. Since the options typically aren't actively traded on an established market, they are deemed to not have an ascertainable fair market value at the time of grant.

What is the tax result of exercising a non-qualified option?

The excess of the fair market value on the exercise date of the stock received over the option price is generally taxable as ***ordinary compensation income.***

The stock receives a tax basis (cost to determine capital gain or loss) of the fair market value on the date of exercise, and the holding period for the stock commences with the date of exercise. If the recipient is an employee, the employer should report the income on Form W-2. If the recipient is not an employee, the company should report the income on Form 1099-NEC (non-employee compensation).

(When the stock is sold during the same year the NQO is exercised and no Form 1099-B is issued by the stock brokerage company for the sale (this is rare), the transaction need not be reported on Schedule D. If the stock brokerage company does issue Form 1099-B for the sale, the ordinary income is reported as part of wages or trade and business income and the sale is reported on Schedule D. The tax basis of the stock is the option price plus the ordinary income reported, usually resulting in no gain or loss or a small loss.)

Special rules apply when the stock received is subject to restrictions that prevent the recipient from selling it. See the explanation below.

Employers are supposed to withhold income taxes for the compensation reported for exercising non-qualified stock options. *The federal withholding is computed based on the rate for bonuses, which is 22% (37% for "supplemental wages" in excess of $1 million) for 2025. Many employees have been surprised to learn they owe additional income taxes on April 15 following the year of exercise because they are actually in a higher tax bracket. The California rate of withholding for non-qualified stock options and bonuses is 10.23%.* Practically speaking, withholding may be impossible when the stock is not sold or is sold through a broker that is not a transfer agent for the employer.

Depending on the taxpayer's other income, he or she may have an "April surprise" of additional tax due because the withholding when the option was exercised was not enough to pay the total tax liability.

Employee compensation relating to non-qualified options is also subject to employment taxes, including Social Security and Medicare tax. Again, it may be impossible for an employer to collect this tax when an employee has left and exercised an option or when the taxes exceed the employee's other cash income.

Communication is essential between the department that administers the stock option program and the corporate payroll department in order for the corporation to meet its reporting obligations. If they aren't met, the corporation could lose the corresponding tax deduction for the compensation amount.

What rules apply when the stock received is not freely transferable and is subject to a risk of forfeiture?

The income from exercising an NQO isn't reported until the stock received is transferable or is not subject to a risk of forfeiture (becomes vested). Note this is an **or** test, so only one condition is required to be satisfied to be taxable. Stock that becomes vested but is not transferable is taxable.

("Insider" stock that is not freely transferable under SEC Act of 1934 Section 16(b) is considered to be non-transferable and subject to a risk of forfeiture until the restrictions lapse. These insider rules are complex, so consult with a securities lawyer about them if you think you may be an insider under Section 16(b).)

The compensation element is determined when the restrictions lapse. The amount of compensation is the excess of the fair market value of the stock *on that date* over the option price.

If the restrictions will never lapse, the transaction is considered closed and the fair market value of the stock is adjusted to consider the restrictions.

Since this postponement puts a "cloud" of uncertainty over the tax results of the transaction, an election is available to secure the tax results, explained below.

Also see the discussion below about the rules for non-qualified deferred compensation plans that apply to non-qualified stock options.

How can a taxpayer avoid postponing the compensation income until restrictions lapse for stock purchased using non-qualified stock options?

The taxpayer may elect under Internal Revenue Code Section 83(b) to report the ordinary income amount as of the date of exercise of the option. *The election is required even when the income amount is zero and must be made within 30 days after exercising the option!*

The election is made by filing a written statement to the Internal Revenue Service office where the taxpayer files his or her income tax return. The written statement may be IRS Form 15620 or an alternative written form with the same information. A copy of the election statement is also given to the employer. Under final regulations issued by the IRS that are effective for exercises of nonqualified stock options on or after January 1, 2016, a copy of the election no longer is required to be attached to the taxpayer's income tax return.

The election may only be revoked with the consent of the Commissioner of the IRS.

What is the advantage of making the election? If the stock rises in value after the exercise of the option, the gain after the exercise date is taxable as a capital gain, potentially eligible for a 15% or 20% tax rate for a long-term capital gain. The maximum federal income tax rate for ordinary income is 37%. The One Big Beautiful Bill Act of 2025 (OBBBA) extended these tax rates after 2025 permanently.

Long-term capital gains rates generally apply to sales of securities held more than one year. Making the Section 83(b) election "starts the clock" for determining the holding period for unvested stock.

The tax brackets for ordinary taxable income are indexed for inflation. For 2025, maximum federal tax rates apply to married persons filing joint returns with taxable income exceeding $751,600; $365,600 for married, filing separate returns; and $626,350 for heads of households and single persons. The maximum federal tax rate for ordinary income is 37%. The maximum federal tax rate for qualifying long-term capital gains and qualified dividends when taxable income exceeds the thresholds listed in this paragraph is 20%.

See the discussion about the net investment income tax below. This additional tax can increase the maximum federal income tax rate for long-term capital gains to 23.8%. Phase-outs of tax benefits based on income thresholds can raise the effective federal income tax rates even higher.

The federal tax rate for long-term capital gains when taxable income for 2025 (indexed for inflation for future years) is below $600,050 for married, filing joint returns, $ 566,400 for heads of households, $533,400 for single persons, and $300,000 for married, filing separate returns is generally 15%.

Individuals with taxable income less than $96,700 for married, filing joint, $64,750 for heads of household, and $48,350 for single persons and married persons filing separate returns for 2025, indexed for inflation for future years, may qualify for a 0% tax rate for long-term capital gains.

Phaseouts also apply to certain itemized deductions and to personal exemption deductions. The thresholds for the phaseouts are indexed for inflation. For 2017, the thresholds are as follows: for married persons filing joint returns with taxable income exceeding $313,800, $156,900 for married filing separate returns, $287,650 for heads of households, and $261,500 for single persons. These phaseouts slightly raise the effective tax rates for high income taxpayers.

Effective for tax years beginning after December 31, 2025, OBBBA phases out certain itemized deductions when taxable income, with itemized deductions added back, exceeds the thresholds where the maximum income tax rates apply. These phaseouts slightly raise the effective tax rates for high-income taxpayers.

With a variety of income thresholds having different tax effects, it will be important to make tax projections using software that is updated for the latest tax law changes when planning for exercising nonqualified stock options. Taxpayers might have other decisions to make, such as whether to sell other stock, whether to defer compensation, or whether to make a Roth conversion. Working with a tax advisor makes sense to discuss the interplay of these matters in tax planning.

What are disadvantages of making the election? If the stock declines in value after the exercise of the option, the loss after the exercise date is a capital loss. The optionee reports ordinary income without an offsetting ordinary deduction if the value declines. Capital losses are only deductible to the extent of capital gains plus $3,000 per year. Excess capital losses may be carried over to subsequent years.

If the stock appreciates, the corporation loses the tax deduction for the increase in value after the date of exercise.

If the employee has to forfeit the stock back to the company, such as for a termination, the capital loss that can be claimed is limited to the option price paid for the stock. The compensation reported as taxable income when the option was exercised is not added to the tax basis of the stock for a forfeiture.

Limited tax relief for some private company stock options, stock grants and RSUs

Employees with stock-based compensation with employer companies that aren't publicly traded have always had a problem with having taxable compensation without receiving or having access to cash to pay the related income taxes.

The Tax Act and Jobs Act included some tax relief for this situation, effective for options exercised and RSUs settled after December 31, 2017.

Certain employees can make an election under amended Internal Revenue Code Section 83(i) to defer recognition of the amount of income for qualified stock transferred to the employee by the employer. The election is effective for income tax purposes, not for computing FICA (Social Security and Medicare) or FUTA taxes.

The election must be made no later than 30 days after the first time the employee's right to the stock is substantially vested or is transferable, whichever occurs earlier.

When the election is made, the income is taxable for the earliest tax year that includes:

1. The first date the qualified stock becomes transferable, including, for this purpose, to the employer.
2. The date the employee first becomes an "excluded employee". An excluded employee is an individual (i) who is a one-percent owner of the corporation at any time during the 10 preceding calendar years; (ii) who is, or has been at any prior time, the chief executive officer or chief financial officer of the corporation or an individual acting in either capacity; (iii) who is a family member of an individual described in (i) or (ii), or (iv) who has been one of the four highest-compensated officers of the corporation for any of the 10 preceding tax years.
3. The first date on which any stock of the employer becomes readily tradable on an established securities market.
4. The date five years after the first date the employee's right to the stock becomes substantially vested; or
5. The date on which the employee revokes his or her election.

If the election is made relating to a "statutory option" (ISO or ESPP), the option will no longer be treated as a statutory option but treated as a nonqualified stock option.

The taxable amount will still be based on the fair market value on the date of exercise, not on the date the income becomes taxable.

Income tax should be withheld based on the maximum income tax rate for the year the income is included in taxable income. (Currently 37%.)

The employer's deduction for the related compensation is also deferred until the employee is taxable for the income.

The election applies for qualified stock of an eligible corporation. A corporation is eligible for a tax year if: (1) no stock of the employer corporation or any predecessor is readily tradable on an established securities market during any preceding calendar year; and (2) the corporation has a written plan under which, in the calendar year, *not less than 80% of all employees who provide services to the corporation in the US or any US possession* are granted stock options or restricted stock units (RSUs) with the same rights and privileges to receive qualified stock.

Employers are subject to notice, withholding and reporting requirements for the election. The IRS is given discretion to provide transitional relief for these requirements and is supposed to issue guidelines for them.

Note that key shareholders won't get any relief and the participation requirements are very broad, which means this election may not really have a wide application. New stock compensation plans will have to be created to meet the requirements.

What are the tax results if the option is sold before it is exercised?

If the option is sold or otherwise disposed of in an arm's length transaction, the money plus the fair market value of any property received is taxable as ordinary compensation income.

In addition, if the transaction is not arm's length, such as a sale to certain related persons, when the person who buys the option exercises it, the original option holder will also recognize ordinary compensation income for the fair market value of the stock received over the amount paid. The person who bought the stock receives a basis adjustment for the income reported by the service provider in the year of exercise. (See item 5.)

For example, Jane sells an option she received from her employer, XYZ Corp., to her daughter, Joanne, for $1,000 in 20X1. During 20X2, Joanne exercises the option. The option price is $4,000. The fair market value on the exercise date of the stock received is $10,000. Joanne sells the stock during 20X3 for $20,000.

Jane has taxable ordinary compensation income for 20X1 of $1,000, the amount received from Joanne.

Jane has taxable ordinary compensation income for 20X2 of $5,000 – the $10,000 fair market value of the stock received less Joanne's $1,000 investment in the option and the $4,000 option price.

Joanne has a capital gain in 20X3 of $10,000 – the $20,000 sale price less her original $1,000 investment in the option, the $4,000 option price and the $5,000 ordinary income reported by Jane in 20X2. (The holding period for the stock begins on the date of exercise of the option. But see the section above relating to stock subject to restrictions for transferability and a risk of forfeiture.)

(The IRS regards arm's length transfers to family members as abusive tax-avoidance transactions, which must be disclosed as "listed transactions" on the optionee's income tax return.)

What if the employer is acquired, resulting in a buy-out of the options or an exchange for new options?

If an acquiring party purchases the outstanding non-qualified stock options from employees or service providers, the money plus the fair market value of any property received by the employees or service providers is taxable as ordinary compensation income.

The IRS has ruled that no taxable income resulted when a company was reorganized in a tax-free reorganization and non-qualified stock options for the new company were issued in exchange for outstanding stock options of the old company.

Should I make gifts of non-qualified options for estate planning? What is the tax impact of doing this?

In some circumstances, it is advantageous to make gifts of non-qualified options or restricted stock. Before going ahead, be sure such transfers are permitted under the terms of the option or the stock restrictions.

Making gifts of these options or stock could have an *estate tax* advantage of shifting future appreciation to your donee.

Please be aware that gifts of employee stock options that have not vested are considered to be incomplete until the shares are vested. The IRS ruled in Revenue Ruling 98-21 that when an employee cannot exercise an option until the employee provides additional services to the employer, the transfer of the option to a donee is not a completed gift until the later of (1) the transfer date or (2) the time when the donee's right to exercise the option is no longer conditioned on the employee's performance of services.

For example, Jill Smith gives non-qualified employee stock options for 300 shares of Tech stock on June 30, 20X1 to her daughter, Judy. The value of the options on June 30, 20X1 is $0. In order for the shares to vest, Jill must work three years after June 30, 20X1 at Tech. The gift will not be considered to be completed until June 30, 20X4. If the value of the options has increased to $200,000 on June 30, 20X4, that will be the value of the completed taxable gift.

It is unclear whether the IRS intends to apply this ruling to transfers before the date the ruling was issued: May 4, 1998.

The election to treat the transfer as completed, discussed above relating to avoiding postponing compensation income, does not apply for gift tax purposes. If the option is exercised and the stock is subject to a risk of forfeiture, the gift is not a completed gift.

Gifts of a present interest in property (generally, not in trust) of up to $19,000 per year (for 2025. Indexed for inflation for future years.) per donee, per donor are exempt from gift tax. Gifts in excess of the $19,000 per year annual gift tax exclusion are subject to gift tax, after applying the lifetime estate and gift exemption.

In most cases, the gift should be substantial to justify the expenses required to value the stock or options for gift tax reporting.

Under OBBBA, the lifetime estate and gift tax exemption, $13,990,000 for 2025, indexed for inflation for future years, is permanent. The tax rate that applies for estates and accumulated taxable gifts exceeding $13,990,000 is subject to a federal tax rate of 40%. Some states also have estate and gift taxes to consider.

The unused estate and gift tax exemption of a spouse who was deceased after December 31, 2010 is "portable" and might be available for the surviving spouse under complex rules. Widows or widowers whose spouse was deceased after December 31, 2010 should consult with a tax advisor about the details, including the requirement to file a federal estate tax return on time.

Making these gifts does not eliminate the *income tax* consequence for the donor. When the donee exercises the option, the donor who originally received the option will still be subject to tax on the ordinary income amount. (Ltr Rul 9722022.) The tax basis of the donee will be increased for the ordinary income recognized by the donor.

If the donor is deceased at the time the option is exercised, the ordinary income will be taxed to the holder of the option as income with respect of a decedent. (If a charity receives nonqualified stock options as a specific bequest, the income will escape income tax.)

Restricted stock does not receive a "fresh start" basis adjustment like other inherited property.

See also the explanation above about sales to related persons.

Planning to sell the stock.

Since the stock is generally treated as acquired on the date of exercise for its fair market value, you should only keep it to the extent it fits in your portfolio.

In other words, would you make an investment in this stock anyway?

If you sell it on the date of exercise, you should have little or no gain or loss except the ordinary income, which you can't avoid.

Considering the risk involved, there are very few cases where having most of your net worth concentrated in stock received from exercising non-qualified options makes sense. An exception is an early exercise of start-up company stock when a lot of appreciation is expected after the option is exercised.

Remember the general rule for tax reporting is shares that can't be identified are accounted for on a first-in, first-out basis. A taxpayer can overcome this rule by giving the broker written instructions to sell specific blocks of stock, such as "sell the 500 shares of Supercorp Stock I acquired on April 15, 20X1." Identifying shares sold as those with the highest tax basis can result in a substantial reduction of the current income tax. A proposal for the Tax Cuts and Jobs Act of 2017 to repeal this election was not passed.

Cash flow requirements may also dictate the sale of stock, including the requirement to pay taxes.

Estimated tax considerations.

The optionee should avoid potential penalties for underpayment of estimated tax or underwithholding by monitoring his or her estimated tax deposits and withholding.

Generally, for federal tax purposes, taxpayers must deposit at least the last year's tax in order to have "protected estimates." Individuals with adjusted gross income for the prior tax year of more than $150,000 ($75,000 for married, filing separately) must deposit a 110% of the prior year's tax to have "protected estimates."

(Some states, including California, don't have "protected estimates" in some circumstances. For example, in California, taxpayers who have more than $1 million of adjusted gross income are required to pay estimated taxes based on the income for the current year. See your tax advisor for details.)

What if I move to another state after receiving a non-qualified stock option, but exercise the option after moving?

You could be subject to tax on the exercise in both states, with a state tax credit available to reduce the impact of double taxation.

Earned income, such as wages or consulting income, is generally taxable in the state in which the services are provided. Some states, such as California, tax residents on income received from all sources. A state tax credit is usually allowed by one of the states to reduce the hardship on the taxpayer.

Multiple-state tax issues are complex. You should consult with a tax advisor if you have this situation.

What is the impact of the rules for non-qualified deferred compensation plans on non-qualified stock options?

The tax laws for non-qualified deferred compensation plans were radically changed by the American Jobs Creation Act of 2004, enacted on October 22, 2004. The IRS has issued comprehensive guidance in final regulations for Internal Revenue Code Section 409A (T.D. 9321).

Under these rules, non-qualified stock options (NQOs) issued with an option price below the fair market value of the stock on the date of grant (in the money) are deemed to be deferred compensation arrangements. The same concept applies to stock appreciation rights (SARs), which are beyond the scope of this discussion. Since most NQOs don't meet the requirements for non-qualified deferred compensation plans, NQOs that were "in the money" at grant will be subject to a 20% penalty tax plus interest from the date of grant to the date of exercise.

The IRS issued Chief Counsel Advice 201521013 on December 18, 2014, outlining the consequences of pricing nonqualified stock options below fair market value on the grant date. In the CCA, income is determined annually for vested stock options. The income is the excess of the fair market value for the stock over the option price, less any income that was previously reported. A 20% penalty plus interest is computed for the income amount.

NQOs that were exercised **and vested** before January 1, 2005 are grandfathered and not subject to the penalty tax. Under transitional rules, employers could "fix" old NQOs by December 31, 2008 (except for certain backdated options – see below) so that employees could avoid the penalty tax. If employees exercised a NQO priced below fair market value on the date of grant that vests after December 31, 2004 **before** the employer "fixed" the option agreement to comply with the new rules, the penalty tax could apply.

NQOs issued by publicly-traded companies usually were issued at fair market value. The fair market value for non-public companies (like Google before its IPO) is harder to determine, so those plans might require modification.

See your plan administrator to find out whether it's safe to exercise your NQOs that vested after 2004 and whether your plan has been amended to comply with these rules.

Generally, non-public companies will need to have an appraisal done within 12 months before a NQO is issued to determine the fair market value of the stock. Alternatively, a non-public company can use a valuation formula in some circumstances. (Consider getting a ruling for the formula.) Start-up corporations with illiquid stock may make a good-faith valuation of their stock with a written report substantiating how required factors were taken in consideration. (With the liability considerations involved, getting an appraisal is recommended.)

Incentive stock options and employee stock purchase plans are exempt from the new rules for non-qualified deferred compensation plans.

The final deferred compensation regulations are a nail in the coffin for non-qualified stock options for non-public companies.

Companies that adopt non-qualified stock option plans should be sure they are in compliance with the rules to avoid having employees be subject to penalties.

Disallowed compensation deductions expanded for publicly-traded corporations

The tax deduction for compensation of certain key executives of public corporations is limited to $1 million per year. In the past, compensation relating to employee stock options was excluded from this limitation as "performance-based compensation."

Effective for tax years beginning after December 31, 2017, the exception for "performance-based compensation" has been repealed. There is a grandfather rule for written plans that were in effect on November 2, 2017, and that are not modified in any material respect on or after that date. The limit applies to any employee of a publicly held corporation who (1) is the principal executive officer (PEO) of the corporation, or acting in that capacity, at any time during the tax year; (2) is the principal financial officer (PFO) of the corporation, or acting in that capacity, at any time during the tax year; (3) is one of the three highest compensated officers for the tax year (other than the PEO or PFO); or was a covered employee of the corporation or any predecessor for any prior tax year beginning on or after January 1, 2017.

Effective for tax years beginning after December 31, 2025, OBBBA has extended the limitation to an allocated portion of $1,000,000 for a covered employee of a publicly-traded member of a controlled group. (An overall $1,000,000 deduction limit applies for the group.)

This limitation could result in the disallowance of significant deductions of compensation relating to the exercise of stock options.

What are the tax consequences for backdated options?

Here are four tax issues of concern for backdated options:

First, incentive stock options (ISOs) and employee stock purchase plans (ESPPs) may only be granted to employees. (IRC §§ 422(a)(2), 423(a)(2).) If the employer backdated the employee's start date, the individual may not have actually been an eligible employee. Therefore, the option will not qualify as an ISO or ESPP, and will be taxed as a non-qualified stock option.

Second, ISOs and ESPPs are required to be priced based on the fair market value on the grant date (or exercise date for ESPPs). (IRC §§ 422(b)(4), 423(b)(6).) If the option fails the pricing test on the actual grant date, it will be taxed according to the rules for non-qualified stock options.

Third, if a non-qualified stock option has an option price less than the fair market value on the grant date, the option is probably subject to the rules for non-qualified stock options under § 409A. (Treasury regulations § 1.409A-a(b)(5)(i)(A).) This means the income from the option will be subject to a 20% penalty tax plus interest.

Fourth, a stock option with an option price less than the fair market value on the grant date won't qualify as "performance-based compensation" for the $1 million limitation of deduction of compensation paid to a covered employee of a publicly-held corporation. (Regs § 1.162-27(e)(2)(vi)(A).) Effective for tax years beginning before January 1, 2018, the limit applies to the CEO and the four highest-paid officers other than the CEO. Applying the limitation would result in the disallowance of significant deductions of compensation relating to exercising stock options. For tax years beginning after December 31, 2017, see the above discussion, "Disallowed compensation deductions expanded for publicly-traded corporations."

Conclusion

Getting professional assistance for managing non-qualifying stock options is a worthwhile investment to get expert tax guidance and help in making sound investment decisions. Since stock prices can be volatile, making decisions based on tax consequences alone can be risky. Those decisions should be based on sound investment practices.

6

Employee Stock Purchase Plans

Employees are often surprised when I tell them that employee stock purchase plans (ESPPs) are a type of stock option. They are defined as a type of "qualified stock option" plan in the Internal Revenue Code. The reason they are options is the employee can elect to participate in the plan or not to participate.

ESPPs and incentive stock options (ISOs) are the two "qualified" stock option plans because they qualify for special tax benefits. Every other stock option plan is taxed under the rules for non-qualified stock options (NQOs).

ESPPs are different from ISOs and NQOs because, in order to qualify, they must have broad employee participation requirements. In other words, they must be non-discriminatory. The only employees who may be excluded are (A) employees who have been employed less than two years, (B) employees whose customary employment is 20 hours or less per week, (C) employees whose employment is for not more than 5 months in any calendar year, and (D) certain highly compensated employees. No employee can be granted an option if, immediately after the option is granted, the employee owns 5% or more of the combined voting power or value of all classes of stock of the employer corporation, its parent or its subsidiary.[1]

1 Internal Revenue Code § 423(b)(3)

The Basics - What are the benefits of Employee Stock Purchase Plans (ESPPs)?

Employees may receive up to a 15% discount, based either on the fair market value of the employer stock on the grant date or the exercise date. If the price under the ESPP is based on the fair market value as of the grant date, the employee participates in the appreciation of the employer stock, without an outlay of cash, until the option expires. No income is reported when the employee purchases stock under the plan. If the employee meets the holding period requirements, any gain over the initial discount (determined on the grant date) is reported as a long-term capital gain, eligible for the 20% maximum federal tax rate.

The option price for an ESPP must be at least the lesser of (a) 85% of the fair market value of the stock on the grant date, or (b) 85% of the fair market value of the stock on the date of exercise.[2] The option price for an ISO may not be less than the fair market value of the stock on the grant date.[3]

Since the Financial Accounting Standards Board has said that no compensation needs to be reported on a company's financial statements provided ESPP options are priced with a discount from fair market value on the grant date of 5% or less from the market price, that may become a new standard for pricing these options.[4] (So far, companies seem to be continuing to use the 15% discount.)

An employee may be granted ESPP options that may initially be exercised for up to $25,000 of stock of the employer corporation, its parent or its subsidiary. The limit is based on the fair market value of the stock on the date of grant.[5]

---

2 Internal Revenue Code § 423(b)(6)

3 Internal Revenue Code § 422(b)(4)

4 Statement of Financial Accounting Standards No. 123 (revised 2004), ¶ 12

5 Internal Revenue Code § 423(b)(8)

An ESPP option generally expires five years after the grant date.[6] In some cases, an ESPP option will expire 27 months after the grant date.[7]

What is the tax result when the holding period requirements are met?

When the holding period requirements are met and the option price is at least 85%, but not more than 100%, of the fair market value of the stock on the dates of grant or exercise, the employee reports the discount determined as of the grant date as ordinary income when the stock is sold or transferred, or at the employee's death. (Note the amount taxable as ordinary income may be different from the actual discount – the excess of the fair market value on the exercise date over the option price – realized by the employee.) When the selling price of the stock is less than the benchmark fair market value, the ordinary income is limited to the excess of the selling price over the option price.[8] The tax basis of the ESPP shares is increased by the ordinary income.[9] Employers typically do not report the ordinary income on Form W-2 for the discount element when the holding period requirements have been met. There is no corresponding tax deduction to the employer for the amount reported as ordinary income by the employee.[10]

When the holding period requirements are met, the excess of the selling price of the stock over the tax basis of the stock (option price plus ordinary income) is taxed as a long-term capital gain, subject to the 20% maximum federal long-term capital gains rate plus the 3.8% net investment income tax.

What is the net investment income tax?

The net investment income tax (NII tax) is a separate 3.8% surtax on the lesser of "net investment income" or the excess of "modified" adjusted

---

6 Internal Revenue Code § 423(b)(7)(A)

7 Internal Revenue Code § 423(b)(7)(B), Treasury Regulations § 1.423-2(h)

8 Internal Revenue Code § 423(c)

9 Internal Revenue Code § 423(c), Treasury Regulations § 1.423-2(k)(2)

10 Treasury Regulations § 1.423-2(k)(1)(ii)

gross income over $250,000 ($125,000 for married taxpayers filing separate income tax returns). Since the NII tax is a separate surtax, it isn't included in the "regular tax" amount when computing the minimum tax credit. (See below for an explanation of the alternative minimum tax.)

The ordinary income from the disqualified disposition of stock acquired by exercising an incentive stock option or an employee stock purchase plan is considered to be "wages" and is not included in net investment income. The ordinary income reported for a qualified disposition of stock acquired from an employee stock purchase plan is a also considered to be "wages". These "wages" are also statutorily excluded from income subject to employment taxes like Social Security and Medicare taxes. This is an advantage of ordinary income from a disqualified disposition of an incentive stock option or an employee stock purchase plan compared to an exercise of a nonqualified stock option.

Most long-term capital gains from securities sales, including long-term capital gains from a qualified sale of stock acquired from exercising an incentive stock option or an employee stock purchase plan, are considered investment income for computing the NII tax.

What happens if the holding period requirements aren't met?

If the holding period requirements aren't met, it is called a disqualifying disposition. In that situation, the disposition is treated like a disposition of stock acquired using a non-qualified option, but the ordinary income is postponed until the year of sale.[11]

If the stock is sold in a disqualified disposition for more than the fair market value on the date of exercise, ordinary compensation income will be reported for the excess of the fair market value on the date of exercise over the option price. Any excess of the sales price over the fair market value on the date of exercise is taxed as a capital gain. The compensation income should be reported on the employee's Form W-2.

---

[11] Internal Revenue Code §§ 423(a), 421(b)

The employer receives a tax deduction for this amount. (If the wages of the employee are capitalized to inventory or a capital asset, the income from the early disposition of an ESPP may also be capitalized.)

If the stock is sold in a disqualifying disposition for less than the fair market value on the date of exercise, there is no provision limiting the ordinary income based on the selling price. *There is no "escape hatch" like for ISOs.* Ordinary income is reported based on the excess of the fair market value of the stock on the exercise date over the option price. The employee reports a capital loss for the excess of the fair market value on the date of exercise over the net sales proceeds. The employee could report ordinary income taxed at 37% and have a capital loss limited to capital gains plus $3,000 – not a good combination. The best remedy is for the employee to generate short-term capital gains to use the capital loss.

Since ESPPs are "qualified stock options," the ordinary income isn't subject to federal income tax withholding or employment taxes, including Social Security, Medicare and federal unemployment taxes.

What is a disqualifying disposition?

Generally, the rules for disqualifying dispositions are the same for ISOs and ESPPs. (The grant date is often called the "subscription date" for ESPPs.) A sale or transfer of the stock before the holding period requirements of more than two years after the grant date and more than one year after the exercise date is a disqualifying disposition. A property division incident to a divorce is not a "transfer." Neither is an inheritance after a death.

Are there any alternative minimum tax (AMT) considerations?

Since ESPPs are a broad-based employee benefit, there are no AMT adjustments for the exercise of ESPP options or the sale of ESPP shares.

May the employee pay for ESPP shares by exchanging other employer shares?

There is no provision permitting a stock swap to exercise an ESPP option.

Some planning considerations.

Since the 15% discount is essentially a gift from the employer, employees generally should participate in an ESPP to the full extent available. If the stock is publicly traded, the employee always has the choice of immediately selling the stock to cash out the income element. If, under the price formula specified in the plan, the option price goes "underwater" (the option price may exceed the fair market value of the stock), the employee should not exercise the option.

The maximum tax benefit of meeting the holding period requirements is the difference between the maximum regular tax rate (currently 37%) and the maximum rate for long-term capital gains, (currently 15% or 20%) plus a potential net investment income tax of 3.8% when modified adjusted gross income exceeds $250,000 for joint filers ($200,000 for singles and $125,000 for married persons filing a separate return).

If the stock is volatile, the employee could lose more than the tax savings by holding the stock. Further, if the stock is sold in a disqualifying disposition for less than the fair market value on the date of exercise, the employee will report ordinary income based on the excess of the fair market value on the date of exercise over the option price, with a capital loss that could be limited to $3,000. Not a good situation.

If the holding period requirements are met and the stock is sold with resulting significant long-term capital gains, the employee could be subject to the alternative minimum tax. The same tax rates apply to long-term capital gains when computing the regular tax and the alternative minimum tax. Effective for 2018 through 2024, the Tax Cuts and Jobs Act of 2017 reduced or eliminated itemized deductions that previously would have been added back to taxable income when computing the alternative minimum tax. The alternative minimum tax was also essentially doubled. This means fewer taxpayers will probably be subject to the alternative minimum tax, but it should still be computed when making planning computations.

OBBBA has made the tax deduction changes of the TCJA permanent, with some changes. Effective for 2025, the deduction for state income taxes and property taxes (SALT) is increased to $40,000 ($20,000 for married, filing a separate return). For 2026, the deduction will be $40,400 ($20,200 for married, filing a separate return). The ceiling will be increased to 101% of the previous year amount for 2027 through 2029, and revert to $10,000 ($5,000 for married filing a separate return) after 2029.

The SALT cap is reduced to no less than the $10,000 ($5,000 for married, filing a separate return) or the actual amount, if less, by 30% of the excess of the taxpayer's modified gross income over $500,000 ($250,000 for married, filing separately) for 2025, and $505,000 ($252,500 for married filing separately) for 2026. The SALT cap phaseout threshold will be increased to 101% of the dollar amount in effect for the previous year for 2027 to 2029.

Since any alternative minimum tax relating to a sale of ESPP shares does not relate to a timing difference, no minimum tax credit will be available relating to the sale.

The ESPP plan for many employers is an automatic payroll deduction plan. This can be a deadly combination with an ISO when the stock price is dropping. If the employee sells ISO shares to use the "escape hatch," but ESPP shares are purchased within 30 days before or 30 days after the sale of the ISO shares, the employee may lose the benefit of the "escape hatch" for shares equal to the number of ESPP shares purchased, under the wash sale rules. See the sections on disqualifying dispositions and the escape hatch in the chapter on incentive stock options.

For example, John Employee sells 1,000 shares of Employer ISO stock for $10,100 on December 10, 20X1. He exercised the ISO on January

1, 20X1, when the fair market value of the stock was $100,100. The option price was $100 (10¢ per share). John made this move to eliminate an AMT adjustment of $100,000, or possibly about $28,000 of federal AMT, in exchange for $10,000 of ordinary income, or about $3,700 of regular tax. Under the company ESPP, John purchases 100 shares Employer stock on November 30, 20X1 and another 100 shares on December 31, 20X1. Under the wash sale exception, John will only be able to use the escape hatch for 800 shares. He will report $20,000 ordinary income for 200 shares plus $8,000 of ordinary income for 800 shares, or a total of $28,000 ordinary income and about $10,360 in income taxes. The tax basis of the ESPP shares will be increased for the disallowed loss for 200 ISO shares of $2,020 – ($20 cost + $20,000 ordinary income) = -$18,000.

Employees tend to accumulate ESPP shares until they represent a large concentration of value in their portfolios. As with any investment, it generally doesn't make good investment sense to have a concentration of investment risk. Employees should have a regular investment strategy of diversification.

Each ESPP purchase represents a separate transaction to be accounted for. Just keeping track of the shares and the related tax attributes is a major chore. It can be practically impossible for an employer to keep track of all of the ESPP history for every employee.

Since there are a wide variety of prices and holding periods of ESPP shares, there can be significant tax advantages of specifically identifying shares to be sold that have the lowest tax bill resulting from the sale

Estimated tax and withholding

Since there are minimal AMT consequence of buying ESPP shares, planning estimated taxes and withholding is less complex than for ISOs. However, since employers don't withhold income taxes relating to the ordinary income from early dispositions and there can be significant tax liabilities from qualifying sales, estimated tax and withholding are still important issues to consider.

The American Jobs Creation Act of 2004, enacted October 22, 2004, included provisions that income realized as the result of exercising an incentive stock option or from an employee stock purchase plan is not subject to employment taxes or income tax withholding.[12] This is a major advantage of "qualified options" compared to non-qualified stock options.

(Some states, including California, don't have "protected estimates" in some circumstances. For example, in California taxpayers who have more than $1 million of adjusted gross income are required to pay estimated taxes based on the income for the current year. See your tax advisor for details.)

[12] American Jobs Creation Act of 2004 § 251(a), Internal Revenue Code §§ 421(b), 423(c), 3121(a)(22), 3231(e)(12), and 3306(b)(19)

7

Stock Grants and RSUs

More employers are using stock grants because stock option plans have become more expensive with changes in financial reporting from Statement of Financial Accounting Standards 123, Sarbannes-Oxley compliance requirements, and new tax compliance requirements under Internal Revenue Code Section 409A.

Since stock grants are a form of non-cash compensation that may not be liquid (especially for companies that don't have publicly-traded stock), *receiving them can result in taxable income without having the cash to pay the tax.*

Stock grants can be restricted stock awards, where you actually receive shares of stock, or restricted stock units or RSUs, which involve issuing credits that will be issued as stock when they vest. RSUs are book entries and not actual shares of stock. Most of the following discussion is related to restricted stock awards, which I will call "stock grants." See the final paragraph below about RSUs.

What are the economic advantages of using stock grants to an employer?

An employer is able to compensate employees and other service providers with no out-of-pocket costs. The employer receives a tax deduction for the fair market value of the stock on the grant date or the vesting date, if the employee doesn't make a Section 83(b) election. (See below.)

(Note the tax deduction for compensation of certain key employees of publicly traded corporations may be limited to $1 million per year.)

The administration expenses for stock grants are the lowest for any equity-based type of compensation. I guesstimate that administration costs for an ISO or NQO might be $1,000 *per grant per year until exercised.* That figure might be low. Consider the legal fees to create a proper stock option plan. Consider creating procedures and documentation to avoid a claim of backdating. Consider the valuation gyrations (Black-Scholes, Bernoulli Lattice models…) you need to go through for financial reporting of stock options, to get answers that professional accountants and financial analysts disagree about. Consider the requirement for non-public companies to have valuation studies performed for their stock on a regular basis in case an option is granted or exercised, or the stock vests after exercise. Consider keeping track of whether options have been exercised or not, grant dates, vesting dates, whether a Section 83(b) election was made, option prices and fair market values when exercised or vested.

I hate to say it, but stock options are a royal pain in the rear for companies that grant them.

The very simplest, low-cost equity-based compensation is a fully-vested stock grant. Not only that, the statute of limitations for tax reporting in case you make a mistake is closed about three years after the filing date for the year of making the grant. Isn't that great?

Stock grants and non-qualified stock options can both be given to non-employees, such as corporate directors and independent contractors. The corporation can literally print its own money if its stock is considered valuable.

What are the economic advantages of stock grants to an employee or service provider?

The intention is for the employee to be motivated to help the company be successful since the employee has an ownership interest in the company.

This is clearly not as great of an advantage as for a stock option, because the employee makes a cash investment in the amount of taxes that must be paid for receiving the grant. This isn't required for stock options until the options are exercised.

The employer's "selling point" of grants to employees is you can't have an "underwater" grant. Many stock options have become worthless when the employer stock value falls. Big Lots was a painful example of a company that offered RSUs to many employees and crashed. The stock may be more likely to keep *some* value than an option, but the upside potential is much more limited and the financial risk is greater.

For publicly-held stock, the employee may be losing a choice about making alternative investments. A grant is taxed somewhat like receiving a cash bonus that is immediately invested in employer stock. Maybe that's not the choice the employee would prefer to make.

For non-public companies, the stock grant may be one of a very limited number of ways an employee can get the stock. The problem is a lack of liquidity and a lack of control. You can't sell it and you might have a very limited say in what happens with the company. Stock grants of non-public company stock are more attractive when you can foresee a liquidity event – going public or being acquired – in the near future. See below about an election to postpone paying the tax for certain grants of stock by companies whose stock isn't publicly traded.

What are the tax results of receiving a stock grant?

If the stock is fully vested when received, the grant is taxable based on the fair market value of the stock on the grant date. The income is taxable as ***ordinary compensation income***. The stock receives a tax basis (cost to determine capital gain or loss) of the fair market value on the grant date, and the holding period of the stock commences with the grant date. If the recipient is an employee, the employer should report the income on Form W-2. If the recipient is not an employee, the company should report the income on Form 1099-Miscellaneous.

Special rules apply when stock is received subject to restrictions that prevent the recipient from selling it. See the explanation below.

Employers are supposed to withhold income taxes for the compensation reported for stock grants. *The federal withholding is computed based on the rate for bonuses, which is 22% (37% for "supplemental wages" in excess of $1 million) for 2025. Many employees have been surprised to learn they owe additional income taxes on April 15 following the year of exercise because they are actually in a higher tax bracket. The California rate of withholding for non-qualified stock options and bonuses is 10.23%.* Practically speaking, withholding may be impossible when the stock is not sold or is sold through a broker that is not a transfer agent for the employer.

Employee compensation relating to stock grants is also subject to employment taxes, including Social Security and Medicare tax. Again, it may be impossible for an employer to collect this tax when the taxes exceed the employee's other cash income.

Stock grants weren't eligible for the $1 million limitation of employer deductions by publicly traded corporations, like stock options were. The exemption for performance-based compensation was generally repealed for tax years beginning after December 31, 2017 by the Tax Cuts and Jobs Act of 2017, but grandfather rules apply. See "Disallowed compensation deductions expanded for publicly-traded corporations" in the chapters on Incentive Stock Options and Nonqualified Stock Options.

Communication is essential between the department that administers the stock grant program and the corporate payroll department in order for the corporation to meet its reporting obligations. If they aren't met, the corporation could lose the corresponding tax deduction for the compensation amount.

What rules apply when the stock received is not freely transferable and is subject to a risk of forfeiture (isn't vested)?

The income from receiving a stock grant isn't reported until the stock received is transferable or is not subject to a risk of forfeiture (becomes vested). Note this is an **or** test, so only one condition is required to be satisfied to be taxable. Stock that becomes vested but is not transferable is taxable.

("Insider" stock that is not freely transferable under SEC Act of 1934 Section 16(b) is considered to be non-transferable and subject to a risk of forfeiture until the restrictions lapse. These insider rules are complex, so consult with a securities lawyer about them if you think you may be an insider under Section 16(b).)

The compensation is determined when the restrictions lapse. The amount of compensation is the fair market value of the stock *on that date*.

If the restrictions will never lapse, the transaction is considered closed and the fair market value of the stock is adjusted to consider the restrictions.

Since this postponement puts a "cloud" of uncertainty over the tax results of the transaction, an election is available to secure the tax results, explained below.

How can a taxpayer avoid postponing the compensation income until restrictions lapse for a stock grant?

The taxpayer may elect under Internal Revenue Code Section 83(b) to report the ordinary income amount as of the grant. *The election is required even when the income amount is zero and must be made within 30 days after receiving the grant!*

The election is made by filing a written statement to the Internal Revenue Service office where the taxpayer files his or her income tax return. A copy of the election statement is also given to the employer. IRS Form 15620 may optionally be used to make the election.

The election may only be revoked with the consent of the Commissioner of the IRS.

What is the advantage of making the election? If the stock rises in value after the grant, the gain after the grant date is taxable as a capital gain, potentially eligible for a 20% tax rate for a long-term capital gain. The maximum federal income tax rate for ordinary income is 37%.

In addition, a 3.8% Medicare Tax on "investment income" when modified adjusted gross income exceeds $250,000 for joint filers ($200,000 for singles and $125,000 for married persons filing a separate return) has been enacted to help pay for Health Care Reform, effective after 2012. So the maximum tax rate for long-term capital gains is 23.8%

What are disadvantages of making the election? If the stock declines in value after the exercise of the option, the loss after the exercise date is a capital loss. The optionee reports ordinary income without an offsetting ordinary deduction if the value declines. Capital losses are only deductible to the extent of capital gains plus $3,000 per year. Excess capital losses may be carried over to subsequent years.

If the stock appreciates, the corporation loses the tax deduction for the increase in value after the grant date.

If the employee has to forfeit the stock back to the company, such as for a termination, no capital loss is allowed except for any amount the employee paid for the stock – usually zero. The compensation reported as taxable income when the option was exercised is not added to the tax basis of the stock for a forfeiture.

Limited tax relief for some private company stock options, stock grants and RSUs

Employees with stock-based compensation with employer companies that aren't publicly traded have always had a problem with having taxable compensation without receiving or having access to cash to pay the related income taxes.

The Tax Act and Jobs Act includes some tax relief for this situation, effective for options exercised and RSUs settled after December 31, 2017.

Certain employees can make an election under amended Internal Revenue Code Section 83(i) to defer recognition of the amount of income for qualified stock transferred to the employee by the employer. The election is effective for income tax purposes, not for computing FICA (Social Security and Medicare) or FUTA taxes.

The election must be made no later than 30 days after the first time the employee's right to the stock is substantially vested or is transferable, whichever occurs earlier.

When the election is made, the income is taxable for the earliest tax year that includes:

1. The first date the qualified stock becomes transferable, including, for this purpose, to the employer.
2. The date the employee first becomes an "excluded employee." An excluded employee is an individual (i) who is a one-percent owner of the corporation at any time during the 10 preceding calendar years; (ii) who is, or has been at any prior time, the chief executive officer or chief financial officer of the corporation or an individual acting in either capacity; (iii) who is a family member of an individual described in (i) or (ii), or (iv) who has been one of the four highest-compensated officers of the corporation for any of the 10 preceding tax years.
3. The first date on which any stock of the employer becomes readily tradable on an established securities market.

4. The date five years after the first date the employee's right to the stock becomes substantially vested; or
5. The date on which the employee revokes his or her election.

If the election is made relating to a "statutory option" (ISO or ESPP), the option will no longer be treated as a statutory option but treated as a nonqualified stock option.

The employer's deduction for the related compensation is also deferred until the employee is taxable for the income.

The election applies for qualified stock of an eligible corporation. A corporation is eligible for a tax year if: (1) no stock of the employer corporation or any predecessor is readily tradable on an established securities market during any preceding calendar year; and (2) the corporation has a written plan under which, in the calendar year, *not less than 80% of all employees who provide services to the corporation in the US or any US possession* are granted stock options or restricted stock units (RSUs) with the same rights and privileges to receive qualified stock.

Employers are subject to notice, withholding and reporting requirements for the election. The IRS is given discretion to provide transitional relief for these requirements and will issue guidelines for them.

Note that key shareholders won't get any relief and the participation requirements are very broad, which means this election may not really have a wide application. New stock compensation plans will have to be created to meet the requirements.

Planning to sell the stock.

Since the stock is generally treated as acquired on the grant date for its fair market value, you should only keep it to the extent it fits in your portfolio.

In other words, would you make an investment in this stock anyway?

If you sell it on the grant date, you should have little or no gain or loss except the ordinary income, which you can't avoid.

Considering the risk involved, there are very few cases where having most of your net worth concentrated in stock received from a stock grant makes sense.

Remember the general rule for tax reporting is shares that can't be identified are accounted for on a first-in, first-out basis. A taxpayer can overcome this rule by giving the broker written instructions to sell specific blocks of stock, such as "sell the 500 shares of Supercorp Stock I acquired on April 15, 20X1." Identifying shares sold as those with the highest tax basis can result in a substantial reduction of the current income tax.

Cash flow requirements may also dictate the sale of stock, including the requirement to pay taxes.

Estimated tax considerations.

The person who receives the stock grant should avoid potential penalties for underpayment of estimated tax or under-withholding by monitoring his or her estimated tax deposits and withholding.

Generally, for federal tax purposes, taxpayers must deposit at least the last year's tax in order to have "protected estimates." Individuals with adjusted gross income for the prior tax year of more than $150,000 ($75,000 for married, filing separately) must deposit a 110% of the prior year's tax to have "protected estimates."

(Some states, including California, don't have "protected estimates" in some circumstances. For example, in California taxpayers who have more than $1 million of adjusted gross income are required to pay estimated taxes based on the income for the current year. See your tax advisor for details.).

What is the impact of the rules for non-qualified deferred compensation plans on stock grants?

The tax laws for non-qualified deferred compensation plans were radically changed by the American Jobs Creation Act of 2004, enacted on October 22, 2004. The IRS has issued preliminary guidance for the new rules in Notice 2005-1 and more comprehensive guidance in final regulations for Internal Revenue Code Section 409A (T.D. 9321).

Stock grants are specifically excluded from these rules. (Hooray!)

Restricted Stock Units (RSUs)

As I explained in the introduction to this chapter, restricted stock units or RSUs are not actual shares of stock, but bookkeeping entries. The stock is issued as the shares vest.

Since RSUs aren't shares of stock, they aren't "property," so the income amount isn't determined until the stock is actually issued. This means that a Section 83(b) election can't be made when an RSU is issued.

In addition, since the RSUs represent compensation to be paid in the future, they are considered to be a form of non-qualified deferred compensation, so they are subject to Section 409A. Since RSUs usually have a predetermined payout (as they vest), they shouldn't be subject to the 20% penalty tax. Employee discretion relating to accepting an RSU and the timing of vesting should be avoided in these plans, because it could subject the employee to the penalty tax.

Conclusion

Getting professional assistance for managing stock grants is a worthwhile investment to make sure you take home the most money possible and make sound investment decisions.

8

Qualified Small Business Stock Gain Exclusion

Before the adoption of the One Big Beautiful Bill Act of 2025 (OBBBA, H.R. 1, P.L. 119-21), noncorporate taxpayers could exclude from taxable income capital gains from the sale or exchange of qualified small business stock held for more than five years.

Before the change, the exclusion was (still applies for qualified stock acquired before July 5, 2025):

- 100% of the gain for qualified stock acquired after September 27, 2010;
- 75% of the gain for qualified stock acquired after February 17, 2009 and before September 28, 2010; and
- 50% of the gain for qualified stock acquired before February 18, 2009 (increased to 60% of the gain attributable to periods before 2019 if the stock was issued by a corporation in an empowerment zone and acquired after December 21, 2000.)

For stock acquired before September 28, 2010, 7% of the excluded gain is a tax preference item for alternative minimum tax reporting.

Excludable gain on dispositions of qualified stock from any single issuer for a tax year is limited to the greater of (1) $10 million, reduced by the aggregate amount excluded for the issuer's stock in prior years ($5 million for married, filing separately); or (2) 10 times the taxpayer's adjusted basis in all of the issuer's stock disposed of during the tax years.

Gains on dispositions of qualified stock held by a pass-through entity for more than five years is passed through to partners, shareholders and participants who held interests in the entity when it acquired the stock and at all times thereafter. The exclusion can't reflect any increase in the person's share of the entity after the entity acquired the stock.

In addition to the exclusion, taxable gains from sales of qualified stock may be deferred under Internal Revenue Codes Section 1045 by reinvesting the sale proceeds in stock of another qualified small business within 60 days after the sale.

Qualified small business stock is stock issued after August 10, 1993, and acquired by the taxpayer at the original issue, directly or through an underwriter, in exchange for money or property, or as compensation for services provided to the corporation. The issuing corporation must be a domestic C corporation other than a regulated investment company, cooperative, or other pass-through corporation.

Both before and immediately after the qualified stock is issued, the corporation's aggregate gross assets must not exceed $50 million, with parent-subsidiary controlled groups treated as one corporation. During substantially all of the taxpayer's holding period, at least 80% of the value of the corporation's assets must be used in the active conduct of qualified trades or businesses.

A qualified business does not include the performance of services in the fields of health, law, engineering, architecture, accounting, actuarial science, performing arts, consulting, athletics, financial services, brokerage services, or any trade or business if its principal asset is the reputation or skill of employees. Hospitality, farming, insurance, finance and mineral extraction also are not qualified businesses.

Note that retail, manufacturing, and research to develop a product are qualifying businesses.

How OBBBA changes the thresholds

OBBBA changes the gain exclusion by creating tiers, effective for stock issued or acquired and to tax years commencing after July 4, 2025. The exclusion ratios are 50% after three years, 75% after four years, and 100% after five years. The per-issue dollar cap for post-enactment shares is increased from $10 million to $15 million reduced by the aggregate amount excluded for the issuer's stock in prior years ($7.5 million for married persons filing separately), indexed for inflation after 2026. The post-enactment aggregate-asset ceiling is increased from $50 million to $75 million, indexed for inflation after 2026.

There is no alternative minimum tax preference for the excluded gains for these shares.

The higher asset ceiling means the stock of more corporations will qualify for the exclusion.

Shareholders who have capital gains from sales of qualified small business stock will be eligible to exclude more of their gains from taxable income.

The holding period requirement to qualify for a partial exclusion has been relaxed, so more sales of qualified small business stock will qualify for some exclusion from taxable income.

In the past, the thresholds haven't been indexed for inflation. Under OBBBA, the thresholds will be automatically increased for inflation after 2026.

Family tax planning tip

Giving family members cash to purchase qualified small business stock can increase the exclusion threshold for the family. (Up to $15 million per family member.)

Choice of entity considerations

Making a decision about what form a business should be requires having a long-term horizon and a crystal ball.

According to a Bureau of Labor Statistics report in 2024, about 20% of startups that opened for business in 2013 failed during the first year. About 39% of startups failed within the first three years. About 50% of startups failed within the first five years. About 65% failed within the first ten years. It seems the odds are against realizing a gain from the sale of startup stock. Only a handful of shareholders do.

For small business stock to qualify for the exclusion, it must be issued by a corporation that qualifies when the stock is issued. The corporation that issues the stock must be a regular "C" corporation (including an LLC that elects to be taxed as a C corporation – most don't). Stock issued by an "S" (passthrough entity) corporation doesn't qualify, but stock issued by a former S corporation after terminating its S election and becoming a C corporation can qualify.

Why is this important?

Business startups typically generate losses during their first few years. Losses of a C corporation are "locked" in the business and aren't deductible for its owners. Losses of passthrough entities are eligible to be deducted on the income tax returns of their owners, subject to limitations like basis limitations, passive activity loss limitations, and at risk limitations.

Owners of general partnerships and sole proprietorships include their shares of "at risk" debt in their investment for the limitation for deducting business losses. (If the business fails, they are liable for the debt.)

Passthrough entities aren't subject to double taxation, like C corporations. The owners pay income taxes on the entity's taxable income and add that income to their tax basis (cost for computing taxable gain) for the sale of their ownership interest.

Partnerships and sole proprietorships have an advantage of being able to possibly liquidate by distributing their assets tax-free.

For businesses whose business plans don't include having a public offering of their shares or selling the business at a multiple asset value for the foreseeable future, these are good reasons to choose passthrough structures, not C corporations.

For businesses that are adequately capitalized and are developing significant intellectual property or significant net income for a high multiple valuation that is expected to be sold soon after five years, or that plan to make a public offering of their shares, C corporations look more attractive.

Employee Stock Options and the Qualified Small Business Stock Capital Gain Exclusion

The Ninth Circuit Court of Appeals has confirmed the Tax Court in holding employee stock options don't qualify as stock for the Small Business Stock Capital Gain Exclusion. The court also ruled the holding period of employee stock options before exercising them isn't included for the 5-year holding period requirement. The shares must be owned to start the clock.[13]

Any ordinary income for stock acquired by exercising an employee stock option isn't eligible for the Small Business Stock Capital Gain Exclusion.

As explained below, determining when the holding period begins becomes complicated when employee stock options have a vesting schedule and the employer or other option granter permits an early exercise of employee stock options. For nonqualified stock options, the employee may elect under Section 83(b) to treat the early exercise as taxable for regular tax and alternative minimum tax reporting. When that election is made, the holding period starts on the date of exercise.

[13] *Natkunanathan v. Commissioner*, 110 AFTR 2d 2012-5193, July 12, 2012.

When that election isn't made, the holding period starts on the later of the vesting date or the date of exercise.

For incentive stock options, the regular tax holding period starts on the date of exercise, regardless of vesting. The Section 83(b) election to treat the early exercise as taxable only applies for the alternative minimum tax and the option is treated as a nonqualified option for alternative minimum tax reporting. (The holding period might start on different dates for regular tax and AMT reporting. Note there is no AMT adjustment relating to most Small Business Stock Capital Gain Exclusions. For stock acquired before September 28, 2010, 7% of the excluded gain is a tax preference item for alternative minimum tax reporting.)

Options Comparison Chart

(As of 8/26/2025. Be alert for changes in the law.)

	NQO	ISO	ESPP
Non-discrimination rules apply?	No	No	Yes
Can be granted to non-employees?	Yes	No	No
Option price limitations based on FMV at grant or exercise?	Yes, under rules. for nonqualified deferred and limits on deduction of compensation for high paid employees of public companies.	100% FMV at grant.	85% FMV at grant or exercise.
Generally taxable at grant?	No	No	No
Generally taxable at exercise for regular tax reporting?	Yes	No	No
Generally AMT adjustment at exercise?	No	Yes	No
AMT basis adjustment for sale?	No	Yes	No
Ordinary income limitation (escape hatch) applies for disqualifying position in year of exercise?	No	Yes	No (Could result in ordinary income and capital loss)

	NQO	ISO	ESPP
Ordinary income when holding period requirements are met?	N/A	No	Yes. Discount from fair market value based on grant date price is ordinary income when stock is sold.
Federal income tax, FICA and Medicare withholding currently required for ordinary income for employee?	Yes	No	No
General result of early exercise (stock ownership not vested)?	Not taxable until vested based on FMV at that date.	No AMT adjustment until vested based on FMV at that date.	N/A
Other restrictions – SEC Rule 16(b)	Postpones taxation not met, lapses.	No AMT adjustment until restriction lapses based on FMV at that date. If holding period not met, ordinary income is recognized based on FMV when restrictions lapse.	If holding period not met, ordinary income is recognized based on FMV when restrictions lapse.
Effect of § 83(b) election for early exercise or SEC Rule 16(b)	Stock transfer treated as complete. General rules above apply for regular tax and AMT.	Stock transfer treated as complete. General rules above apply for regular tax and AMT.	Stock transfer treated as complete. General rules above apply for regular tax and AMT.
Disqualified disposition if stock disposed of when stock not held more than two years from grant date and one year from exercise date?	No	Yes	Yes
Gift of unexercised options allowed?	Yes	No	No

	NQO	ISO	ESPP
Transfer of unexercised option to family partnership allowed?	Yes[14]	No	No

[14] "Not recommended. The IRS has determined that the use of FLPs with NQOs is abusive. The exercise of an NQO will result in ordinary income to the service provider (employee or independent contractor.) The sale of an NQO to a FLP is also a listed transaction requiring special disclosure. (Temporary Regulations §1.83-7, Treasury Notice 2003-47.)"

Made in United States
Orlando, FL
04 November 2026

90200717R00056